Nonsense on Stilts?
A Quaker View of Human Rights

"Natural Rights is nonsense: natural and impresciptible rights, rhetorical nonsense – nonsense on stilts."
Anarchical Fallacies, Jeremy Bentham (philosopher) 1748 to 1832

Edited by

Nigel Dower

With

Philip Hills & Michael Bartlet

William Sessions Limited
York, England

© The Authors 2008

ISBN 978-1-85072-373-8

Cover illustrations
Women in Black, vigil held in Belgrade, March 2007, commemorating massacre of Albanian civilians by Serb forces in Suva Reka, Kosovo, 26 March 1999.
© Women in Black
Labongo-Layamo camp in Kitgum (northern Uganda)
© IRIN

Printed in Times New Roman
from Author's Disc
by Sessions of York
The Ebor Press
York, England

Contents

Nicholas Sagovsky	Preface	v
	Note on Contributors	vii
	Introduction	1
Frank Cranmer	One Quaker's View of Human Rights in a Socio-juridical Context	3
Michael Bartlet	What can Quakers say about human rights?	17
Philip Hills	Human Rights, Quakerism and the Inner Light	33
Nigel Dower	Human Rights and That of God	43
Roger Iredale	Human Rights: a Practical Approach	53
Harvey Cox	Human Rights in Theory and Practice	61
Alan Pleydell	Quakers, Human Rights and the International Responsibility to Protect (R2P)	75
Judith Baker	International Aspects of Quaker Human Rights Work	95

Preface

Do Christians support human rights? It would be hard nowadays to argue that we do not, but our conversion has been slow and often reluctant. As the impact of developing human rights thinking changes western societies, there are areas in which some churches now wish to distance themselves from the practice of human rights without weakening their commitment to such foundational documents as the Universal Declaration of Human Rights.

The essays in this book demonstrate why Quakers are so deeply committed to the practice of human rights. Quakers do not accept hierarchies. Their prophetic commitment to 'that of God' in everyone is the basis for a radical egalitarianism that challenges every form of division into first and second class citizens and every form of exclusion from citizenship itself. The basis of modern human rights thinking lies in an inclusive citizenship which values all equally.

The Quaker commitment to human rights is based on belief in the inner light – that of God in every human being. This belief has produced an emphasis on conscience and on people's fundamental right to differ. Quakers were, after a long struggle, in the forefront of those who won recognition for the right to refuse the state's call to bear arms. They demonstrated that there were limits to citizenship: the state may command the loyalty of its citizens but not the citizen's conscience.

The radical implications of these Quaker commitments are evident throughout this book. But so are the difficulties raised by the implementation of human rights thinking. We live in a world where many do not appreciate or respect the demands or the privileges of an order based on human rights. In the face of those who flagrantly abuse human rights, as in Darfur or Zimbabwe, it remains extraordinarily difficult to see how a thoroughgoing commitment to pacifism can be maintained. To what extent and on what issues can a conscientious right to opt out of the demands of the state be allowed: if it is granted on the bearing of arms, must it be granted on health and safety legislation? As human rights thinking develops we have to re-visit its basis: for some a basis in religious commitment, for others in secular pragmatism. For how long, and with what strength, can this alliance hold? These are some of the questions raised here.

This is a book for 2008, the sixtieth anniversary of the Universal Declaration of Human Rights. It is by Quakers but it is not merely for Quakers. No doubt there will be Quakers who are encouraged in their commitment to human rights by these essays. Perhaps more importantly, there will be non-Quakers, like myself, who will learn more about the deep and historic roots of the prophetic commitment of Quakers to human rights. These essays remind us of the immense power of a human idea that came into its own in the twentieth century and must remain as a bedrock for our social and political practice in the twenty-first. This is a book for all Friends of Human Rights.

Nicholas Sagovsky
Canon Theologian, Westminster Abbey
January 1, 2008

Notes on Contributors

Judith Baker worked on the QUNO human rights and refugees programme from 1983-1986. She currently clerks the Overseas Peacebuilding Group of Quaker Peace and Social Witness. She is also representative for Quaker Peace and Social Witness on the UK section of the coalition to stop the use of child soldiers.

Michael Bartlet is secretary to Quaker Peace and Social Witness Public Affairs Group. He has previously worked as a barrister and as a teacher in schools, adult education and abroad.

Harvey Cox is from Northern Ireland and is a graduate of Dublin University (Trinity College) and the London School of Economics. He lectured in Politics at Liverpool University and helped establish the Institute of Irish Studies there. He served for several years on the Quaker Peace and Service Northern Ireland committee and its successor, Quaker house Belfast management Committee, as well as on QPS Central Committee and the Public Affairs Group of QPSW.

Frank Cranmer, a government affairs consultant, is a member of the Public Affairs Group of QPSW. He is also a Fellow of St Chad's College, Durham, and an honorary research fellow in the Centre for Law and Religion at Cardiff Law School.

Nigel Dower Honorary Senior Lecturer in Philosophy, University of Aberdeen. He has specialized in issues in global ethics and his publications include *World Ethics – the New Agenda* (EUP 1998; 2007).

Philip Hills is clerk of the QPSW Public Affairs Group. Now retired, he formerly worked as a civil servant and then as Professorial Fellow in Policy Research in Engineering, Science and Technology at the University of Manchester.

Roger Iredale is a member of Mid-Somerset Area Meeting and has travelled extensively throughout Africa, Asia, Latin America and the South Pacific. As emeritus Professor of International Education at the University of Manchester he is keenly interested in relations between the powerful and the oppressed.

Alan Pleydell is Programme Manager Post-Yugoslav Countries for Quaker Peace and Social Witness. He oversees 'Dealing with the Past', local and regional initiatives in unofficial truth and reconciliation work in the western Balkans.

Introduction

This short book arises from consideration by the Public Affairs Group of Quaker Peace and Social Witness. It contains papers written by some members of the Group and by some other Quakers with experience in the field.

The papers, as readers will quickly discover, vary greatly in style and approach. They represent the personal views of the particular authors and do not necessarily reflect the position of the Religious Society of Friends (Quakers) even where such a corporate position exists.

In part, it is this heterogeneity which emboldens us to lay the papers before a wider audience: for it reflects the wide range of views that exist among the Society of Friends on this, as on many other subjects, though all contained within a shared outlook based on a compassionate understanding of human affairs and a commitment to peace.

We hope that readers will find this a timely contribution to issues currently at the forefront both global and domestic affairs.

Nigel Dower
Philip Hills
Michael Bartlet

January 2008

One Quaker's View of Human Rights in a Socio-juridical Context

Frank Cranmer

Abstract

Human rights as currently understood are not rooted in any specifically-Christian tradition. The New Testament evidence reveals attitudes that are impossible to reconcile with current thinking on human rights; and it has even been argued that the notion of human rights arose in opposition to institutional Christianity and oppressive notions of 'divine justice' – though this is by no means undisputed. The key documents relating to human rights are products of the Enlightenment, but much modern discourse on natural law and natural rights continues to be derived from mediaeval scholastic theology, however problematical that may be. Modern Roman Catholic canon law suggests that merely to oppose 'rights' and 'duties' may be to over-simplify a complex web of mutual responsibilities. But in legal, as opposed to moral, terms, unenforceable rights are of little practical value; therefore, though Friends might look elsewhere for a moral basis for human rights, the positivist approach to their day-to-day enforcement should not be lightly dismissed.

A paper in advance of a recent meeting of Quaker Public Affairs Group posed a number of questions about the nature and origins of human rights. Some of the issues raised are basic to any wider discussion of the Society's attitude towards human rights, and it is those that this paper seeks to address.[1]

The origin of human rights

It is clear that human rights are not rooted in any specifically-Christian tradition, since even the most cursory examination of the New Testament evidence reveals attitudes that are impossible to reconcile with current thinking on human rights. When the author of Ephesians wrote 'Slaves, be obedient to those who are your earthly masters...'[2] it obviously did not occur to him that there might be any contradiction between slavery and the Christian faith (and though some modern translations have attempted to soften the blow with 'servants', Ephesians was written in an era when cleaning-ladies were unknown – and the Greek text has the unequivocal *douloi*). Similarly, because the sixteenth century was a different world with very different moral norms, the bloody history of the Reformation and Counter-Reformation makes uncomfortable reading for the modern student of human rights law. But as James Lloyd Carr so rightly observed, 'the Middle Ages were not *us* in Fancy Dress... they believed in Hellfire and the Everlasting Pit';[3] and it was precisely *because* Christians on both sides of the Reformation divide believed that heretics would endure everlasting damnation that they concluded that torture in this life was but a small price to pay for avoiding eternal misery in the next.

In a recent lecture, Lord Bingham of Cornhill took a similar view of the secular nature of human rights, pointing out that the freedom of thought, conscience and religion guaranteed by Article 9 of the European Convention on Human Rights and Article 18 of the Universal Declaration of Human Rights

> ... is a right which, historically, established religions have found it very hard to accommodate and in some places still

do. The reason is not far to seek. Those who believe... that the religion to which they adhere has an exclusive perception of the truth and offers an exclusive path to salvation also tend to believe, naturally enough, both that they should resist any attempt to weaken or challenge that faith and also that they should convert others to it.[4]

The Anglican theologian Nicholas Sagovsky would go even further than Bingham and argue that, far from being part of the Christian tradition, the notion of human rights arose

> ... in *opposition* to the public practice of Christianity, against oppressive notions of divine order and 'divine justice'... It was only ... with the publication in 1891 of *Rerum Novarum*, that the Roman Catholic Church began to promote such 'rights' as an expression of human dignity, and only after the Second World War, with the founding of the World Council of Churches in 1948, that the Protestant and Orthodox Churches found a common voice in support of human rights.[5]

Sagovsky suggests that, in moral terms, a simplistic conception of human rights does not go far enough. He appears to adopt the argument of liberation theologians that 'the justice of God is exercised in support of those who are socially marginalized' and links this with the Jesus of Luke/Acts, who 'reaches out to the marginalized and reintegrates them within the kingdom that celebrates God's jubilee': in short, that Christianity's bias to the poor overrides a strictly egalitarian philosophy of human rights. He concludes, however, that for the churches simply to turn away from the pursuit of human rights in pursuit of an alternative agenda 'seems... little short of a betrayal of humanity in the name of religion...'.[6]

It should be said that the views of Bingham and Sagovsky are by no means undisputed. Robert McCorquodale, for example, argues that

> ... much of the legal and social discourse of human rights is grounded in Biblical material and... the language of human rights is a contemporary discourse that is consistent with the discourse and practice of Christ...[7]

and, inevitably, there is much truth in what he says – if by 'the discourse and practice of Christ' he means 'the ethical content of the teachings of Jesus'. But in so saying he implies, perhaps unconsciously, a dissonance between the Jesus of the Gospels and the teaching and practice of the first-century Church on issues such as slavery that Friends might accept as axiomatic but which many mainstream Christians would wish to reject.

Human rights and natural law

Bingham suggests that the key documents in the evolution of human rights are the American Declaration of Independence 1776, the Déclaration des Droits de l'Homme et du Citoyen 1789, and the first ten Amendments to the US Constitution adopted in 1791.[8] In short, 'human rights' is a product not of religion but of the Enlightenment, which sees human rights as an inalienable consequence of human existence. The proponents of this view rested their case, at least implicitly, on a natural law approach to rights: that by the exercise of reason it could be established that human beings had certain inalienable rights *as human beings*.

Much modern discourse on natural law and natural rights continues to be derived, to a surprising degree, from the writings of Thomas Aquinas,[9] who believed that humankind's natural reason would direct us towards right ends because human nature is rational nature. Aquinas conceived of four types of law:

- the eternal law that is God's plan for us all and which only God can know;
- the natural law that is the rational person's participation in the eternal law;
- the law derived from natural principles (for example, that we should not kill people because we should not harm them); and
- the general principles of law for the guidance of legislators.

The problem with the scholastics' approach, however, is that even on its own terms it is open to two serious objections.

The first is this: if natural law can be deduced by the exercise of reason alone, why is there so much evidence to suggest that, in the real world, is it *not* so deduced? For example, while it is a basic principle of the English law of contract that (unless executed under seal) a contract is only enforceable if it includes an element of consideration on each side, the concept of consideration is completely alien to the Scots law of obligations. If the governing principle of contractual obligations in England is '*quid pro quo*', in Scotland it is 'my word is my bond'; and one cannot help wondering how two mature legal systems can have arrived at such opposite conclusions. At a much more basic level, while there is probably a general consensus that adultery is undesirable, different jurisdictions categorise it in different ways: as a criminal offence (for example, in Saudi Arabia), as a civil wrong (until recently, the position in the Republic of Ireland), or as an activity which while not unlawful *per se* is adequate evidence of marital breakdown for the purpose of divorce proceedings (England and Wales). And on what are generally regarded as matters of morality it is possible for different communities even in the same State to come to quite different results: genital activity in private between consenting males over the age of twenty ceased to be an offence in England and Wales in 1967,[10] *while remaining a crime in Northern Ireland for a further fifteen years.*[11]

The second is perhaps more damaging in terms of the systematic theology that Aquinas himself espoused:[12] if rational humanity tends to pursue right ends, then to what purpose was the Incarnation? And to the obvious counter-argument – that human nature is, at root, morally sound – is dangerously near to realising the Pelagian heresy which Aquinas himself would have rejected. In short, there seems to be a serious mismatch between the concept of 'natural law' and the concept of 'original sin'.

Rights and duties

Rights imply duties; and it is assumed in common law jurisdictions that a right inhering in one legal person assumes a corresponding duty on another; so if, for example, I have an easement/servitude in respect of someone else's land, the landowner has a duty not to obstruct me in the exercise of my right. In a common law context it is almost inevitable that individuals will conflict with each other in the exercise of their private rights and it is ultimately for the courts to adjudicate those conflicts.

But the dichotomy between rights and duties is not necessarily absolute. Significantly, the Roman Catholic *Codex Iuris Canonici 1983* always speaks of 'duties and rights' rather than 'rights and duties'.[13] Therefore, the Roman Catholic model does not proceed exclusively from the common law assumption that if A has a right, B has a corresponding duty; in addition, the *Codex* assumes that a right implies a duty *subsisting in the same person*. In the social theology of *Pacem in Terris*, for example,

... man's awareness of his rights must inevitably lead him to the recognition of his duties. The possession of rights involves the duty of implementing those rights, for they are the expression of a man's personal dignity. And the possession of rights also involves their recognition and respect by other people.[14]

So, for example, the right to free speech implies the duty to speak the truth *with circumspection*.[15] This is quite contrary to the idea of 'playing your hand' espoused by the eminent American jurist John Rawls: 'I'll give you a right if you'll give me a duty'.

A 'neighbour' principle?

In *Donoghue v Stevenson*[16] (the 'snail in the bottle' case), the question at issue was whether, even though a manufacturer had no contractual duty of care to a third party with whom he had no financial relationship, he might still have a duty of care in delict. In addressing the extent to which a person might be liable for damage to another, Lord Atkin, referring back to the parable of the Good Samaritan,[17] enunciated what has become known in some quarters as the 'neighbour principle':

> The rule that you are to love your neighbour becomes in law you must not injure your neighbour; and the lawyer's question 'Who is my neighbour?' receives a restricted reply. You must take reasonable care to avoid acts or omissions which you can reasonably foresee would be likely to injure your neighbour. Who then in law is my neighbour? The answer seems to be persons who are so closely and directly affected by my act that I ought reasonably to have them in contemplation as being so affected when I am directing my mind to the acts or omissions which are called in question.[18]

Has this anything to say to us in the context of how we seek to exercise our human rights? In asserting our own rights, how far may we go before we begin to conflict with the rights of others? Does the principle enunciated by Lord Atkin, potentially at least, imply an element of the 'duties and rights' approach of the *Codex*? For example, is there (or should there be?) some moral limitation on the right to the peaceful enjoyment of possessions under Article 1 of the First Protocol to the European Convention, if 'peaceful enjoyment' means that the rich flourish at the expense of the poor? And does the right of parents under Article 2 of the Protocol (on the right to education) '... to ensure such education and teaching in conformity with their own religions and philosophical convictions' include the right to run fee-paying, independent faith-schools – Friends' schools not excepted – that, coincidentally, tend to confer a degree of social privilege on their pupils?

Human rights as a product of moral norms?

If human rights are not based on natural law or on traditional Biblical teaching, on what *can* they be based? The most obvious answer would seem to be that they are founded on current moral norms: and, over time, those moral norms have moved away from what might have been regarded fifty years ago as 'Christian principles'. Corporal punishment in schools has been outlawed; previous generations had held to the principle 'spare the rod, spoil the child' which was derived from Proverbs 13:24 and 23:13–14. As noted above, homosexual acts between consenting adult males were a criminal offence in England and Wales until 1967; we now have the Civil Partnership Act 2004. On the other hand, the enactment of the Company Securities (Insider Dealing) Act 1985 in response to a series of major financial scandals criminalised an activity that had been previously regarded simply as prudent business practice and (possibly) as the exercise of one's unrestricted right to use one's personal property. Finally, and perhaps most starkly, when the authors of the American Declaration of Independence averred that

> ... all men are created equal, that they are endowed by their Creator with certain unalienable Rights, that among these are Life, Liberty and the pursuit of Happiness...

they neglected to make it clear that, in their view, their Creator had *not*, of course, intended to bestow those blessings on Native or Black Americans.

Conclusion: a Quaker positivism?

That there has been a decisive shift in public policy-making from Judaeo-Christian ethics to a common moral paradigm should not present Friends with any particular problem – whatever difficulties it may cause for certain other religious groups.

The crux of the matter is that in pursuing human rights, religion and law have different ends in view. Part of the role of a religion is to locate rights in the context of *relationships*, not as an impersonal, prescriptive code but as a moral imperative towards the recognition of 'that of God in every person'. But it is axiomatic you cannot make people 'good' by legislation; and legal systems seek, largely, to regulate behaviour in terms of outcomes – acts or omissions – rather than in terms of moral intent. Some recent actions of animal rights activists, for example, which have been undertaken for reasons that the perpetrators regard as entirely moral have nevertheless resulting in criminal sanctions because in English law criminal damage is criminal damage, irrespective of motive.

But in any event, whether the concept of human rights is rooted in the Christian tradition or not, *there is no going back*. One might also reasonably assume that no right-thinking person would want, for example, tribunals that were not 'fair and impartial' within the terms of Article 6 of the Convention. And if, for some obscure reason, someone *did* want tribunals that were partial and unfair, to what conceivable Judaeo-Christian principle could that person appeal for support?

The result of the paradigm shift is that human rights in the United Kingdom are those enshrined in the Human Rights Act 1998 and the European Convention on Human Rights. In United Kingdom law, human rights are essentially positivist; and I would contend that that is both reasonable and proportionate, for two reasons. First, society can only recognise rights when it has agreed what those rights are; and in a society governed by the rule of law, once agreement on a major issue of public policy has been reached, it is normally expressed in legislation of some kind. It is not possible, for example, to create an all-embracing 'right to life' so long as there are deep divisions between those who assert 'the woman's right to choose' and those who hold that the destruction of human life is in all cases wrong. Secondly, the purpose of human rights is to give the citizen redress against public authorities; and it is against public authorities specifically that the Human Rights Act 1998 provides a remedy for breach of Convention rights.[19] Except as an aspiration, the concept of human rights is not very relevant to the day-to-day operation of private law. If my neighbour erects a new fence that encroaches on part of my garden or if someone who owes me money refuses to pay, my most obvious remedy is to sue at common law. On the other hand, if the local authority appropriates my land *ultra vires* and without due process or if Her Majesty's Revenue and Customs overestimates my tax liability and refuses to refund the excess, it may be more effective for me to rely on the right to peaceful enjoyment of possessions under Article 1 of the First Protocol to the European Convention than to bring an action in tort or delict.

In order to be fully effective, human rights need to be enshrined in some kind of basic law that binds public authorities – which is why the European Convention has been a relatively useful tool for enforcement. It has recently been proposed that United Kingdom adherence to the Convention should be supplemented, or even possibly replaced, with a 'British Bill of Rights'; and it seems that the intention of this proposed shift is to provide a basis on which the European Court of Human Rights may give the same margin of appreciation to decisions of the United Kingdom courts as it gives to decisions of the German ones.[20] The difference is, however, that human rights are firmly entrenched in Chapter 1 of the German *Grundgesetz,* or Basic Law, while the British system has no completely tamper-proof method of entrenching legislation.

Much maligned though it may be, positivism has its uses: whatever its potential value as an object of aspiration, a right that is not clearly set out in a justiciable document is for most practical, day-to-day purposes no right at all.[21] Perhaps in developing a response to broader questions of rights and responsibilities Friends might usefully explore two themes: how human rights relate to our recognition of 'that of God in every person' – echoed in McCorquodale's assertion that contemporary discourse on human rights is consonant with the teachings of Jesus – and whether the Roman Catholic canonical concept of rights and duties subsisting together in the same person might have anything helpful to say to us.

Notes

1. I should like to thank Michael Bartlet for commenting on this paper in draft and, in particular, for suggesting that I explore the 'neighbour principle'; however, I must take sole responsibility for the content.
2. Ephesians 6:5. Though the authorship of Ephesians is doubtful, the identity of the author is irrelevant to the present discussion. Whether

or not it was Paul who wrote Ephesians, the mere fact that it was included in the Canon must indicate that the early Church did not disapprove of its sentiments.
3. *The Harpole Report*, 1984, Harmondsworth: Penguin, p. 131.
4. 'Endowed by their Creator?' (2005) 37 Ecc LJ 173–185, p. 181.
5. Sagovsky, Nicholas (2002), 'Human Rights, Divine Justice and the Churches', in Mark Hill (ed.), *Religious Liberty & Human Rights*, Cardiff: University of Wales Press, p. 46.
6. 'Human Rights, Divine Justice and the Churches', pp. 58, 61, 65.
7. 'Contemporary Human Rights and Christianity', 2005, *Law & Justice* 154 6–26, p. 8.
8. 'Endowed by their Creator?' in 2005, 37 Ecc LJ 173–185, p 183. Somewhat surprisingly, he does not mention Tom Paine's *The Rights of Man* published in 1791–92.
9. See, for example, John Finnis: *Natural Law and Natural Rights*, 1980, Oxford: Clarendon Press.
10. Sexual Offences (Amendment) Act 1967 s 1.
11. It was decriminalised by the Homosexual Offences (Northern Ireland) Order 1982.
12. And which, it should be noted, I emphatically reject.
13. For example, Canon 96: 'By baptism one is incorporated into the Church of Christ and constituted a person in it, with the duties and the rights [*officiis et iuribus*] which, in accordance with each one's status, are proper to Christians…'
14. Angelo G Roncalli: *Pacem in Terris* para 44 (*Acta Apostolicae Sedis* 55 (1963), pp. 257–304).
15. For example, Canon 218 declares that 'Those who are engaged in the sacred disciplines enjoy a lawful freedom of inquiry and of prudently expressing their opinions on matters in which they have expertise, while observing a due respect for the teaching [*magisterium*] of the Church.'.
16. [1932] AC 532.
17. Luke 10:25–37.
18. [1932] AC 532 at 580. This was subsequently modified by *Caparo Industries Plc v Dickman and others* [1990] 1 All ER 568; [1990] 2 WLR 358 into a three-stage test: that the damage is foreseeable, that there is a relationship of proximity or neighbourhood, and that

the situation is such that it would be fair, just and reasonable that the law should impose a duty of a given scope on one party for the benefit of the other.
19. Human Rights Act 1998 s 6(1): 'It is unlawful for a public authority to act in a way which is incompatible with a Convention right'.
20. But perhaps one contributory factor in the general decline of politicians' enthusiasm for the human rights agenda might be, at least in part, the tendency since the commencement of the Human Rights Act 1998 for the courts to elevate Convention rights above the administrative preferences or convenience of government.
21 Jeremy Bentham made this point much more forcefully in his *Anarchical Fallacies*: 'That which has no existence can not be destroy'd: that which can not be destroy'd can not require any thing to preserve it from being destroy'd. Natural rights is simple nonsense: natural and imprescriptible rights, rhetorical nonsense, nonsense upon stilts': Philip Schofield, Catherine Pease-Watkin and Cyprian Blamires eds: *Rights, Representation, and Reform – Nonsense upon Stilts and Other Writings on the French Revolution*, 2002, Oxford: Clarendon Press 2002, p 330.

What can Quakers say about human rights?

Michael Bartlet

Abstract

An early conception of human rights is implicit in the seventeenth century political and religious experience of Friends. Such rights are inherent in the 'neighbour principle,' as a source of social responsibility, common to world faiths. Human rights are conceptually interconnected and from a religious perspective may be grounded in a right to freedom of conscience and worship. Difficulties arise where Human rights are abstracted from concrete social situations. Rights are best considered as correlative to responsibilities and necessarily rooted in human relationships. While not in themselves a panacea to social and legal problems, they are a useful currency in building legal and political accountability in a shared international community. While human rights are neither uniquely Quaker or confined to a Judeo-Christian tradition they nevertheless resonate with authentic Quaker experience.

The 'human' aspect of human rights is too often disregarded. Any meaningful approach to human rights involves an intuition about what it means 'to be' human prior to any moral claim about the human good such 'being' implies. For Quakers this approach or understanding requires attentiveness to our history, and the claim that this history has on us today. It requires also a sensitivity in our current practice and discipline, to a wider pluralistic society, where the language of human rights is itself one of the ties that bind society together.

Michael Bartlet

One distinctive dimension of a Quaker understanding of human rights is the legacy of participation in the seventeenth century English Revolution. Early Quakers articulated an astonishing set of political claims inspired by a religious insight that every individual has the capacity for experience of God. The writing and thinking of George Fox and Gerald Winstanley, involved breathtaking claims – both moral and political, to freedom of conscience, jury trial, universal franchise, abolition of the death penalty, political equality of women, public ownership of land and an end to religious taxation (tithes). The development of an early language of rights, forty years prior to the English Bill of Rights, is itself remarkable. The moral claim to universal franchise prefigured its political realisation by over 250 years.

Attentiveness to this radical tradition suggests that a Quaker understanding of what it means to be human, and hence the rights implied by that humanity, is both broader and deeper than the consensus of mainstream Christianity. Such an understanding of rights is inscribed in Quaker testimonies to equality, justice, peace, truth and simplicity. Equality, in its ample sense, amounting to a claim to political participation and empowerment that goes far beyond 'equality before the law', both to challenge hierarchies of decision-making and claim equality of access to social and economic goods. Early expressions of such rights are aspirational and prophetic rather than pragmatic and legally entrenched.

In writing of the four aspects of our central work, *Quaker Faith and Practice* includes 'raising awareness and developing understanding within and without Britain Yearly Meeting about the basic tenets of Quaker faith and practice such as spirituality, peace and human rights.'[1] Yet while, from this, human rights would seem to be central to an understanding of what we do centrally, QF&P contains few specific references to them. The references use the expression in the popular sense of implying a moral claim, on

What can Quakers say about human rights?

account of our common humanity. Human rights are referred to in the context of homelessness,[2] slavery,[3] the peace tax campaign[4] and in a statement of London Yearly meeting of 1986:

> *In the end human rights are about people being treated and feeling like people who matter. We are reminded graphically of violations of human rights far away and near at hand. In ignorance or knowingly we all violate human rights. We are all involved in the exercise and the abuse of power.*[5]

Although human rights are treated as axiomatic to Quaker thinking, the language of human rights presents problems from both a political and religious perspective. In part there is a problem of terms. Human rights describe both what 'is' and 'ought' to be. They describe both aspirational – or even prophetic – claims on a society from the basis of an understanding of humanity, and those fundamental human norms, that are legally recognised as entrenched against the fickleness of political change. While the two are clearly connected, 'rights' without remedies are empty rhetoric. Such a remedy assumes a duty – or responsibility – usually on the state, to provide that remedy.

A clear philosophy of human rights requires a coherent theory or theology of the state. For a dissenting tradition, with an ambivalent relationship with the secular state, it is hard to anchor duties in a body to which only conditional allegiance is recognised. In addition human rights are often expressed as civil and political rather than social and cultural rights. These conventional human rights ignore 'rights' to food, housing and health care which may be more meaningful to the everyday experience of the majority of people in the developing world and more significant to the poorest. Without the basic security of shelter and adequate water and food, all other expressions of human rights appear as something of a mockery. There is also an inevitable tension between individual and collective rights. This becomes particularly acute in relation to the environment where collective environmental rights require a strong limitation on the content of individual rights.

Golden Rule

Human rights are both implied by Quaker testimonies, and are equally a common Christian and more broadly religious currency. Their strength is in their universality. While the Old Testament is strong in an emphasis on duties, and the rights of God vis-à-vis his people, the New Testament expresses an optimistic faith in the possibility of human thriving and flourishing which implies foundational rights or goods. The neighbour principle, expressed in the parable of the Good Samaritan[6] provides both a Christian foundation for the development of human rights and a point of convergence with other faiths. In response to the lawyer's questions regarding what he must do to inherit eternal life, Christ refers him to the Jewish Law, which the lawyer cites as:

> Love the Lord your God with all your heart and with all your soul and with all your strength and all your mind'; and, 'Love your neighbour as your self.'[7]

Such an understanding subverts a contractual conception of rights, for it is from the stranger, from whom he has no expectations, that the man who falls among thieves receives neighbourliness. This is close to a sense of right simply on the basis of our humanity.

The Golden Rule, is common to all great world faiths. It is expressed in the compassion of the Buddha, the Hindic sense of neighbour as ourself, or the insight of Rabbi Hillel: 'What is hateful to you do not do to your neighbour. This is the whole Torah; all the rest is commentary'.[8] It is expressed in the saying of Confucius "do not do to others what you do not want done to yourself,"[9] and in Muhammad's 'None of you has faith until you love for your neighbour what you love for yourself' and in his farewell sermon: 'Hurt no-one that no one may hurt you.' While Quaker and religious faith implies human rights, such rights from a humanist can be derived equally from an understanding of the intrinsic value of life rooted in a common humanity that need not be limited by theistic faith.[10]

Content of human rights

What would be the content of rights derived from an intrinsic human and religious identity? An apt starting point might be that of freedom of conscience and worship. For Quakers, in the seventeenth century, a right to worship, including the right to listen to God,[11] developed into a claim to resist the powers of the state in compelling the bearing of arms or the administration of oaths. A right to 'freedom of conscience', implies a right to 'manifest' that conscience as an expression of identity. It also implies a right to share and inform that conscience in the community of the faithful. This in turn requires an understanding of equality, for we all, potentially, share the same capacity for experience of God. From this derives expectations or rights that are held simply by virtue of humanity, and thence logically a respect for the rights of minorities to 'manifest' their collective conscience. But conscience is more than an individual and internal faculty, etymologically (Latin, *conscire* – to know with) it is a corporate collective concept.[12] Whether understood individually or collectively, from the right to manifest conscience flow the rights of free speech, association and civil liberty.[13]

Other human rights can be firmly anchored in these religious insights. The value of each individual underpins the profound reverence for life informing both a pacifist abhorrence of the taking of life[14] and a commitment to justice, peace and the integrity of creation. Recognition of what becomes a 'human right' to life starts here. The rights to a fair trial and not to be tortured, stem from a regard both that conscience should never be coerced and from the need for the protection of the integrity of the person, whether from state violence or individual aggression. But a religious perspective is only one possible starting point for the existence of human rights. For a humanist they might start with a sense of the dignity and worth of each human being. From the neighbour principle we could equally well start with the right to basic security of the person, health, housing and education. The significance is the profound interconnectedness of different rights as aspects of a wider integrated whole.

Snails and ginger beer

In a famous case in the 1930's concerning the profound shock received by a woman on finding a live snail in a bottle of ginger beer, Lord Atkin used the Golden Rule to *create* new rights. In *Donoghue and Stevenson* (1932), he defined a legal 'duty of care', stemming from the neighbour principle of the Gospels. In his famous judgment he cited the parable in saying,

> The rule that you are to love your neighbour becomes in law, you must not injure your neighbour; ... Who then in law is my neighbour? The answer seems to be – persons who are so closely and directly affected by my act that I ought reasonably to have them in contemplation as being so affected when I am directing my mind to the acts or omissions which are called in question.[15]

While in this country human rights have evolved through statute rather than as a branch of the common law, the neighbour principle represents an apt conceptual starting point. In relation to a right to privacy,[16] judges have adopted a similar common law approach to flesh out the application of the Human Rights Act (1998).

Nonsense on Stilts

The moral foundation of human rights need not imply a rejection of a positivist approach to their development. Since a right without a remedy is legally meaningless. A moral claim requires positive political steps to be taken to give it effect. Rights require a state and judiciary to apply and enforce them. Without enforcement they become, in Bentham's words, 'nonsense on stilts'. While we may have responsibility towards our universal neighbour, the substance of that responsibility is socially and culturally specific. Obligations need to be negotiated in the practical and communal activity of democratic politics and the messiness of everyday life. Where social conditions change, so must obligations. The existence of the internet transforms the content of freedom of expression; new technology for surveillance changes an understanding of privacy; and the potential for the extension of our natural lives infuses a 'right to life' with new considerations.

The 'social contract' is a potent metaphor for the communal activity of politics but it lacks the full development of a vision of human rights. The Lockean ideal is expressed in the English Bill of Rights (1689) where natural rights give individuals a reciprocal claim against the state. Rights implicit in the Bill of Rights become explicit in the foundational documents of the French and American revolutions. Both documents represent a fusion of moral and legal rights. The American Declaration of Independence self-confidently asserts 'We hold these rights to be self-evident, that all men are created equal, that they are endowed by their creator with certain inalienable rights, that among these are life, liberty and the pursuit of happiness.' The self-evidence of pursuit of happiness reveals a remarkable optimism in a shared sense of what it means to be human. Human rights have been transformed from the reciprocal claims of a social contract into grace or gift. They become, in a sense prefigured by early Quaker thinking, claims that arise simply by virtue of our human being, that is extrinsic to any reciprocal obligation – even the malefactor has a right to life, the right to liberty is not earned through work.

In a society that accepts that human rights are commonplace maybe the question that needs answering is: what human rights do you believe in? Almost any claim can be formulated in terms of human rights. Human rights have become almost an alternative legal language. Multi-national companies couch claims against taxation in the name of a right to property. Celebrities claim rights to privacy to limit expression on matters of public interest. A right to family life can be used by the wife of Philip Lawrence to argue that his murderer should be extradited, and by his murderer, having served his sentence, that he should be able to remain in the UK. A right to life is used, energetically, on both sides of arguments about abortion and euthanasia.

If there is a specific Quaker, and indeed Christian, inflection to human rights, it is perhaps here. Where human rights become so persuasive as to become a universal legal language, there is a clear place to argue that where these rights are contested there should be a clear direction in favour of the poor, the vulnerable, and excluded minorities. It is not to suggest that human rights can always trump other claims but that they can be a creative way of breathing moral life into an otherwise sterile legal skeleton. It is this sense, I think, that underpins the peace tax campaign – the claim of those with a conscientious objection to the payment of taxation for military expenditure to divert the proportion of taxes spent on defence to other purposes. Here Quakers argue for a very specific interpretation to be given both to a right to life and to freedom of conscience. Human rights here are being used in the aspirational sense. A right to hypothecate taxation is clearly not an existing entrenched right awaiting judicial recognition – it is an argument for a particular political or constitutional arrangement in tension with the collective discernment of priorities that is the basis of a single consolidated fund. There are two contrasting theories of right one quintessentially individual and the other collective.

It is in the very essence of human rights that they have to carry the consent of the surrounding social majority, so it may paradoxically both be right for a Quaker to make such a claim and for a conscientious judge to resist that claim on behalf of democratically made laws. The claim, even if unsuccessful, may be far from futile in that the process or litigating the issue provides a transparent and potentially inspiring challenge to the state. The challenge will be resisted by judges until those challenging the *status quo* can persuade a democratic electorate of the justice of their claim. In a democracy, the recognition of a right of a minority will requires the implicit consent, even if not the active support, of a majority. What for one generation is understood as a political claim (or right in the aspirational sense) for the next may become entrenched as a 'fundamental' right that, as with women's franchise, is legally buttressed against political change. The absence of a process of entrenchment, that goes beyond signing up to international treaties or consent to international norms, provides a cogent argument for a written constitution. While Britain could withdraw from its commitment to the European Convention on Human Rights by a majority in Parliament, a written constitution can require more arduous procedures for amendment of its fundamental provisions.

The image of Justice as a blindfolded deity with a pair of scales offers a metaphor of objectivity in which justice is necessarily separated from relationships and a sense of what is right between people in community. Human rights only take shape in real social situations; here too a focus on the poor, the vulnerable and the excluded is important. Working out what this means is a process that inevitably involves compromise and conciliation. The contingent nature of the process is recognised in the European Convention of Human Rights (ECHR). The ECHR is in turn the foundation for the Human Rights Act (1998) (HRA). While some rights i.e. the right not to be tortured[17] are legally absolute this is not the case with many others. There is, for instance, a boundary where the right to freedom of speech may interfere with another's privacy. Extreme expression of speech may endanger human life. This is recognised in the fact that while the right to life,[18] prohibition of torture, the right to liberty and security,[19] prohibition of punishment without the law[20] are considered absolute, others, such as the rights to the protection of family life,[21] expression,[22] and assembly[23] are qualified,[24] in the sense that they need to be balanced against each other. While the right to freedom of conscience is absolute the right to manifest it may be limited.

Problems

Human rights are inherently contentious. The concept of a human right generally begins in a claim against the state and the limitation of tyranny. As such, a right depends on a state to claim against and a body to exercise that claim. If claims of right outstrip the capacity to realise them, the inflation of the language of rights leads eventually to devaluation or even bankruptcy of the concept itself. In a democratic society rights against a state imply a civil duty to participate politically. Without that duty, claims remain hollow. This is recognised specifically in the African Charter on Human Rights and People's Rights. The relationship between rights and duties is affirmed in its 'First Article:

> The member states of the OAU, parties to the present Charter shall recognise the rights duties and freedoms

What can Quakers say about human rights?

enshrined in the Charter and shall undertake to adapt legislation or other measures to give effect to them.[25]

Where the concept of human rights is extended from claims against a state to claims against a much wider set of public bodies, the difficulties are compounded because those authorities themselves may have rights against the state. The problem is given an additional twist where human rights can be founded against individuals.[26] The recent setting up of the Commission on Equality and Human Rights illustrates some of the problems. An individual's right to free exercise of religion may conflict with equality rights in relationship to both gender and sexuality, or indeed a claim of religious bodies to instil uniformity. While Quakers understand sexuality as an intrinsic aspect of who we are as people and strive to give the same respect to gay and heterosexual members, this is by no means universally accepted in much religious thinking. There can be no purely legal fix to a problem that requires a participative political discussion creating a consensus on the validity and limits of diversity.

Human rights depend on the values of the society in which they are realised. Values have to be contested for those rights to have meaning. A danger here is that so far as human rights are applicable only to a local political ecology they cease to be universal. In so far as they are universal, on the other hand, there is a danger that a stripping away of distinctions can leave us, with 'a view of human beings as bare autonomous selves abstracted from all those relationships which actually make human beings interesting, significant and individual.'[27] While rights are often presented as a counterpoint to duties, responsibilities possibly provide a better correlative. While duties are essentially fixed, responsibilities are negotiated in relationship and point towards a vision of a dynamic process of social mutuality. But these responsibilities can never be merely contractual. While human rights cannot flourish without a responsible society, individual responsibility cannot be the price of entitlement to such a right. It is the vulnerable, above all, who may lack the capacity for responsibility who are most in need of human rights. Individual rights require collective responsibility.

For Quakers, John Macmurray's thinking regarding the form of the personal gives an added dimension to our commitment to the excluded. The content of human rights is realised in the form of the personal and in the messiness of human relationships. If God, as Macmurray suggests, is revealed through relationship, a culture of human rights can only be realised in society i.e. rights cannot simply be abstracted individual claims. In the introduction to *The Form of the Personal*, Macmurray writes, 'All meaningful knowledge is for the sake of action, and all meaningful action is for the sake of friendship.' Only friendship offers the context for the resolution of these tensions. The nature of that friendship is expressed in *Quaker Faith and Practice*: 'In friendship we are beyond law and obedience, beyond rules and commandments, beyond all constraint, in a world of freedom.'[28] He then enigmatically adds 'But did not Jesus say, 'Ye are my friends if ye do whatsoever I command you?' Yes, he did. We on our side are apt to miss the quiet humour of his paradoxes. 'These are our commandments', he goes on, 'that ye love one another'.[29]

Conclusion

While Quaker thinking underpins a strong commitment to human rights, such commitment has to be a part of a much wider consensus: what we can say authentically is necessarily shared. Two dimensions of Quaker insights deserve particular recognition. Friends were among the first to think in terms of rights pertaining simply by virtue of being human. In their seventeenth century insight of 'that of God in everyone', Friends illuminate a spiritual principle that implies everyone's legal rights deserve protection.

Secondly Friends may bring to the table of human rights a particular awareness of and sensitivity to the excluded, born of a historical experience of being a minority. The Universal Declaration of Human Rights (1948) is precisely that – *universal*. It represents an artful political compromise between such Christian principles and the *Golden Rule* as understood in 'humanism' and other faiths. If human rights are to be universal they need, inevitably, to follow the moral contours of a set of shared values. Without serious negotiation of those values there is a danger that a claim of rights can become a rhetorical device that may prevent serious discussion about the nature of those values. Maybe part of the role of Friends in that negotiation is in a little way to show in our own contribution a clear commitment to the vulnerable, the excluded and the poor – those who are in the least powerful position to assert their rights. Can Quakers perhaps inhabit a cross roads or intersection between two communities, being both conversant with a Christian mainstream of which we are a tributary and at the same time, when recognising the claim that our history has upon us, able to speak with authority about an inclusive humanity that respects both cultural minorities and personal diversity?

If human rights have become a common global language it would be churlish not to recognise that as a real progress. A culture of human rights represents a radical departure from the *realpolitik*, blind obedience to the state and social hierarchy that formed the history of much of the twentieth century. The shared values expressed in the rules based system of the Universal Declaration of Human Rights and the UN Charter is a real if tentative achievement. If such universal moral norms are to be effective it would be rather surprising if one faith were to offer insights that are unique. Don't we as Friends, after all, believe that there is that of God, not just in every Friend, but in everyone?

Notes

1. *Quaker Faith & Practice*, 1999, Second Edition, London: Britain Yearly Meeting, 8.02.
2. QF&P 23.23.
3. QF&P 21.49.
4. QF&P 23.28.
5. QF&P 24.49.
6. Luke, Chapter 10, Verses 25 to 37.
7. The parabolic method of teaching here refers the lawyer to knowledge that he already has.
8. Talmud, Shabbat 31a ca. BCE 50 to 10 CE. For this and the subsequent insight, I am indebted to Frank Cranmer.
9. Analects 15.23.
10. Ronald Dworkin, in *Taking Rights Seriously*, 1977, Harvard University Press, refers to 'The institution of rights ... representing the majority's promise to the minority that their dignity and equality will be restricted'.
11. While this was mooted among independents in the Commonwealth, it only became a partial reality in the Toleration Act of 1689 and Catholic emancipation was not achieved until 1829. The Episcopal Church in Scotland was not fully recognised until 1792.
12. See C.S. Lewis, 1960, *Studies in Words,* Cambridge: Cambridge University Press.
13. In so far as there is a distinction between human rights and civil liberties (*Droits du l'homme and droits du citoyen*) civil liberties are the more political concept and have attracted greater hostility both from the executive and the judiciary.
14. Although opinions may differ on whether this is an absolute right that always trumps others and whether a refusal to kill may at time result in more death than the reluctant acceptance of sue of limited force.
15. Donoghue (or McAlister) v Stevenson [1932] ALL ER Rep1; [1932] AC 562 ; House of Lords
16. Where *European Convention on Human Rights* (ECHR) Article 8 right has no statutory analogue in domestic law.

17. Article 3, *European Convention for the Protection of Human Rights and Fundamental Freedoms* (ECHR) Rome, 4, XI 1950.
18. Article 2 ECHR.
19. Article 4 ECHR.
20. Article 7 ECHR.
21. Article 6 ECHR.
22. Article 10 ECHR.
23. Article 11 ECHR.
24. Such qualifications need to be in pursuit of a legitimate aim, in accordance with law, where there is a pressing social need and where the aim is proportionate.
25. *African [Banjul] Charter on Human and Peoples' Rights*, adopted June 27, 1981, OAU Doc. CAB/LEG/67/3 rev. 5, 21 I.L.M. 58 (1982), *entered into force* Oct. 21, 1986.
26. Sometimes referred to as the courts giving them 'horizontal effect'.
27. John Hapgood in his Sydney Bailey memorial lecture (1998), Unpublished.
28. QF&P 22.10.
29. Excerpt taken from, Macmurray, J., 1979, *Ye are my Friends* and *To Save from Fear*, London: Quaker Home Service, p. 4.

Human Rights, Quakerism and the Inner Light

Philip Hills

Abstract

This paper analyses the basis and nature of human rights as exemplified in four of the best known declarations of human rights. It notes the individualistic nature of such rights and the declarations' relative silence on the rights of, and duties to, the wider community. It goes on to examine the possible contribution Quakers might make to such rights, particularly in the context of duties to the communities in which they live. It concludes by suggesting that one such contribution might be to discern and promote a new testimony.

Introduction

This paper examines some of the problems inherent in current formulations of human rights and considers whether Quakers might be able to make a particular or unique contribution to their development.

The Basis of Human Rights

The first modern formulations of human rights emerged towards the end of the eighteenth century, exemplified in the United States' Declaration of Independence (1776) and the Declaration of the Rights of Man (1789), which arose from the French Revolution. Those drafting the declarations claimed as their authority that '[w]e hold these truths to be self-evident, that all men are created equal, that they are endowed by their Creator with certain unalienable rights'.[1] In the French case the rights were similarly declared 'natural, unalienable, and sacred' and proclaimed 'under the auspices of the Supreme Being'.[2]

More recently the United Nations' Universal Declaration of Human Rights (1948) while it refers in its preamble to 'the inherent dignity and ... inalienable rights of all members of the human family' is a great deal more pragmatic. It cites as justification the 'barbarous acts' that have resulted from 'disregard and contempt for human rights'. It goes on to argue 'it is essential, if man is not ... to have recourse ... to rebellion against tyranny and oppression, that human rights should be protected by the rule of law'. It proclaims the declaration as 'a common standard of achievement for all people and for all nations'.[3] The European Convention on Human Rights (ECHR, 1950) is, if anything even more pragmatic.[4]

In reality, from the eighteenth century on, human rights have been proclaimed and entrenched in constitutions as a means of protecting individuals from the encroaching power of the state - power that may, in a formal sense, be perfectly legal. For example, most activities of the Nazi government in Germany may well have occurred within the laws of the Third Reich but would be widely held as denying Germans their more fundamental rights. When entrenched in national constitutions the concept of 'right' tilts the balance to be struck between the interest of the individual and that of the state firmly towards the former. Hence, while human rights may once have been seen as divinely sanctioned, or simply self-evidently natural to the human condition, they are now recognised as based primarily on need.

The Nature of Human Rights

The rights set out in the Declarations of Independence and of the Rights of Man are, almost without exception, of a very high order of generality: rights to life, liberty, equality of treatment, property and security These are repeated in the more recent formulations and there is wide agreement to their inclusion. The Universal Declaration and the ECHR, however, go much further. Many more specific rights are included as, for example, when Articles 25 and 26 of the Universal Declaration invoke rights to social security and universal education. Similarly, the ECHR includes, among others, rights to be considered innocent until proved guilty, to form and join trade unions, to marry, and the right to respect for private and family life.[5]

There is wide agreement on the highly generalised rights, but as the proposed rights become more specific and detailed, they become more subject to challenge. This is reflected in the fact that the Universal Declaration, in particular, proclaims itself to be 'a common standard of achievement for all peoples and all nations'.[6] It is more an aspiration than a prescription.

These relatively recent declarations of detailed rights are the outcome of painful negotiations, even haggling, between national governments. Hence their content tends to be rather qualified by exceptions and attenuated by evident compromises. Moreover, in many parts of the world, the rights are not universally observed, underlining the weakness of rights that lack reliable means of enforcement.

Communal Rights and the Rights of Others

As noted above human rights have been proclaimed as a way of protecting individuals against state power. For that reason they are essentially individualistic, especially at the higher levels of generality. This raises problems. The declarations provide little guidance on how to reconcile different rights when they conflict, or the conflicting rights of different individuals. Does freedom of speech include freedom to indulge in racial abuse? Does the right to own property include the right to own guns? And, how much property? How do we trade off expenditure on social security against the right of access to (and expenditure on) education?

Furthermore, in resisting the encroachment of the state, declarations of rights tend to underplay the interests of the community in other forms. It may be declared that 'liberty consists in the freedom to do everything that injures no one else'.[7] This would include, for example, everybody's right to travel by air as they wish. When one person flies across the world he does not demonstrably harm any other specific individual. Yet if everyone flew too often, all would eventually suffer from increased global warming.

Hence, while generalised proclamations of rights provide some guarantees against the abuse of power by the state, when too strongly insisted upon they may be a charter for selfishness. Yet, when specified in more detail, rights become more liable to conflict with each other and more subject to controversy.

Duties

It is sometimes argued that in return for claiming rights, individuals should have duties specifically laid upon them. In a purely logical sense this is inevitably true: if I have a right to a pension it must mean that someone has a duty to pay me one. Every right that one person enjoys implies a duty on some other person – who may be an individual or some institution such as the state. When I claim a right I argue that there is a rule, or law, that says that someone shall allow me a freedom or do something for me. The right, for example, to trial by jury or to vote in a secret ballot implies laws that oblige the government to organise criminal justice, or elections, in particular ways, and imposes duties on all concerned to facilitate this.

This brings out some of the conflicts that may arise between the rights of different individuals. The rights of the child impose duties on the parents that limit the latter's rights – perhaps to choose their work freely. Sometimes the unborn child's right to life itself has to be balanced against the mother's similar right. The burglar's freedom is limited by the victim's right to own property. Here the formal statements of right do not help much. Indeed, such cases are inevitably coloured by circumstances that formal guidance can never completely anticipate.

It is also sometimes claimed that if a person wishes to claim a right to, for example, unemployment benefit, he has a duty to look for work. This may (or may not) be a moral obligation, but it is not a logical corollary of having the right. The logical corollary of the right is on another person to pay the benefit. In fact, those proclaiming the duty to look for work are actually qualifying, or even denying, the right. They are saying: 'you don't have an unconditional right to unemployment benefit, but you can have the money if you seek a job'.

Quaker Insights

Do Friends have any particular or unique contribution to make to the debate on these matters? In particular, are there unrecognised, or not much recognised, rights we would wish to assert and have we anything to say about communal rights? What are our special insights?

G. M. Trevelyan, captured the essence of Quakerism, describing Friends 'guiding their own lives by a light that was indeed partly the "inner light" in each man and woman, but was also a tradition and a set of spiritual rules of extraordinary potency handed on from father to son and mother to daughter ... The finer essence was surely this – that Christian qualities matter much more than Christian dogmas".[8] That 'finer essence', however, did, and does, stem from the concept of the inner light which is the mode of unmediated communion with God. This, in turn, is the basis for our lack of clergy, creeds, dogma and liturgy.

The concept of the light within has in common with that of human rights an emphatically individualistic approach. It places the interests of the individual firmly ahead of those of the state (and we need to distinguish here between the state and other forms of community). It affirms the well-being of individuals as the ultimate purpose of government. Individuals should not to be sacrificed as a means to wider ends. They are ends in themselves. Lest awareness of a direct relationship with God should lead to hubristic excesses, however, Quakerism deploys, as Trevelyan describes them, 'spiritual rules of extraordinary potency'. These test an individual's insights against the discernment of his or her peers to ensure that they reflect 'Christian qualities'.

What Can Friends Say?

Thus any Quaker contribution to human rights thinking would have a robust individualism in common with, for example, the American Declaration of Independence. It might also include an element deriving from what Trevelyan calls 'Christian qualities', which modern Friends might wish to see, in this context, as a more specific description of community-considering characteristics. For it is our acceptance of that of God, the risen Christ, within *others* – within prisoners, refugees, the homeless and all who are disadvantaged or rejected – that is the basis of Friends' early and sustained preoccupation with social concerns. Our perception of the inner light within *ourselves* and its association with Christ, the man for others, while it affirms the individual, also recognises the highest calling of the individual to be to live, not for him- or herself, but for others.

Thus, in Quakerism the concern for the individual is balanced by concern for others – the community. In fact this extra dimension is encapsulated in the other terms used for the inner light 'that of God' or 'the Christ within' symbolising characteristics such as understanding, compassion and tolerance.

Most Friends would probably accept that this, like human rights, rests on an assertion about what it means to be human and, in Friends' case, an assertion about the nature of God. Many Friends would also argue, however, that it is an assertion confirmed by the experience of working in communities and of personal fulfilment. Friends might agree that the essence of 'God in everyone' is love, and that this offers guidance on the spirit in which to approach human rights.

It may be that our discipline of discernment can help us to see and articulate the needs of the community more clearly while retaining ultimate concern for each individual. We have done this before through our concerns and testimonies, particularly nowadays, those to peace and equality. Perhaps we need more testimonies, or to espouse more concerns, and to preach them. One might be for our life in communities; another for the environment. The following might be a starting point.

Our Life in Community

As Isaac Pennington told us, 'our life is love, and peace, and tenderness; and bearing one with another, and forgiving one another, and not laying accusations one against another; but praying one for another, and helping one another up with a tender hand'.[9]

While we have individual rights in all the communities in which we live, we must exercise them with loving consideration for all, remembering our duty to help others to enjoy those same rights and to help them up with a tender hand.

In a world that exalts individual choice and consumer demand we are called to restraint and to giving, more than to receiving; to courtesy and to consideration; and to a selfless love.

A Concern for the Environment

As we learn more about the world in which we live we come to understand better our place in it. We know now, more than ever before, that such dominion over the earth that we have been granted, or have achieved, is conditional on our exercising that dominion with loving care for all of our environment. We know that failure to exercise that care will not only destroy a place of beauty, but also our place in it.

A New Testimony

These concerns are not, perhaps, in the same category as our traditional testimonies to Truth, Peace, Equality and Simplicity and are, to a large extent, subsumed in those testimonies. There may, however, be a case for a new testimony that would cover them more explicitly: a testimony to Caring.

Notes

1. The unanimous declaration of the thirteen United States of America – In Congress July 4, 1776. Preamble. Library of Congress. Documents of the Continental Congress and the Constitutional Convention 1774 – 1789.
2. Declaration of the Rights of Man and of the Citizen. Approved by the National Assembly of France, August 26, 1789. English edition prepared by Gerald Murphy (the Cleveland Free-Net aa300) and

distributed by the Cybercasting Service Division of the National Public Telecomputing Network.
3. Universal Declaration of Human Rights (UDHR). Preamble. United Nations Department of Public Information. Office of the High Commissioner for Human Rights.
4. Fully titled 'The Convention for the Protection of Human Rights and Fundamental Freedoms as amended by Protocol No. 11' (ECHR). Council of Europe. Published by the European Court of Human Rights.
5. ECHR op.cit., articles 6, 8, 11 and 12.
6. UDHR op.cit., Preamble.
7. Declaration of the Rights of Man, op.cit. Article 4
8. Trevelyan, G.M., 1950, *Illustrated English Social History* Vol.2, London. Longmans, Green and Co, p.125.
9. Isaac Pennington 1667 – quoted in *Quaker Faith and Practice*. Chapter 10. Section 01. Third Edition. The Yearly Meeting of the Religious Society of Friends (Quakers) in Britain. 2005.

Human Rights and That of God

Nigel Dower

Abstract

In this paper I argue that it is natural for Quakers to support Human Rights. Given our belief in answering that of God in everyone, we can support human rights law –nationally and internationally – and also the development of human rights thinking at an ethical level, in that these will lead to greater answering of the that of God in all. Though the language of that of God and of human rights is rather different, both provide a universalistic ethical framework and both can be seen as supporting a form of 'global ethic' as an ethic which can be endorsed from many different 'starting points' – secular, religious, Kantian, Christian, Buddhist etc. 'That of God' discourse also supports this, but it is a starting point that only a few of us use.

Several of the chapters in this book examine the relationship between Quaker beliefs and human rights thinking.[1] I am broadly sympathetic to the approaches taken by these authors that there is a broad consonance between Quaker thought about that of God in everyone and the motivation behind the advocacy of human rights, but that there are problems intellectually with the idea of human rights both now and in the history of thought. But my approach to these issues is somewhat different.

If we ask the question 'should Quakers be in favour of the idea of human rights and of their increasing acceptance?', there might be several different ways in which this could be answered. We can consider it first at the legal/sociological level, second at the ethical/theoretical level. First, in regard to the existence of human rights law both at national levels, at regional levels, and at international levels, as well as the existence of what may be called a human rights culture in societies, it is fairly clear that most Quakers, if not all Quakers, would support the existence and development of these in general. Of course particular laws or particular implementations of laws may have unfortunate consequences, and these need to be criticised and opposed, but there is little doubt that the general development of human rights law and culture both protects and advances human goods in a way that most Quakers would acknowledge as answering that of God in everyone. I will come back to this level later, because there are further qualifications needed, but now want to turn to the more basic level – the level of ethical and/or metaphysical claims associated with human rights thinking.

Should then Quakers be in favour of a claim – an ethical claim – that all human beings have human rights which ought be protected, promoted and respected by everyone else? Here there is more room for reasonable disagreement amongst Quakers, but before I indicate this, a further distinction is necessary. Quakers could support human rights thinking either because they thought that the Quaker belief in that of God in everyone *is itself a claim* about the rights which everyone has; or, less ambitiously, because, whilst the belief in that of God in everyone is not itself a human rights claim, nevertheless the existence and development of human rights thinking amongst others supports the same common shared global ethic which is needed in order to address the human problems which we face.

For me, possibly because I am a philosopher, this is an important distinction which needs clarifying. In order to make the distinction I need to make a general point about the idea of a shared ethic.

An ethic – that is a set of values and norms accepted by a person or a group – may be supported for a number of different reasons. Thus the common rules of morality may be supported by a Christian, a Muslim, a humanist, a utilitarian or a Kantian.[2] These include norms about not lying, not stealing, helping other and so on. Their worldviews or theories may be rather different, but what each person has reason to support may be various values and norms which others support for other reasons. This does not mean of course that there is total agreement about how to apply these values and norms, but there is sufficient convergence for us to talk of a shared ethic.

Now this point is very relevant to the way we think of a global ethic. By a global ethic I mean an ethic which postulates both some universal norms and values and some trans-boundary obligations towards everyone in the world. For instance most thinkers would accept that there are the positive universal value of health and the negative universal value of extreme poverty or hunger; the duty anywhere not to lie, coerce or steal; and the trans-boundary responsibility for the rich in one part of the world to help the very poor in another part of the world. Given that a global ethic may well be an ethic which is shared by many all over the world – and we each have plenty of reasons for wanting there to be such an ethic – it is particularly pertinent to note how much difference there might be in different worldviews which support any shared global ethic that might develop.[3]

Now it is clear that human rights claims at the ethical level are indeed global ethics claims. That is, a human rights ethic is a species of global ethic. The claim we have human rights is a claim about the moral status of all human beings as human beings, with an understanding that we have responsibilities towards one another in a global ethical community. It is also clear that human rights claims constituted a global ethic in the second sense I indicated of being an ethic widely shared by many thinkers throughout the world.

What I think should be equally clear is that while many thinkers would say they believed in human rights, the reasons why these thinkers make these claims may in fact be rather different. And here many of the points made in other chapters are very relevant to understanding that diversity of approach. As they point out, many thinkers will see human rights as either products of natural law or themselves natural rights, others will see them as God-given, others see them as some kind of product of social contract and so on.

There are in fact a number of modern philosophical theories, each subtly different from the others, which also support claims that all human beings have human rights. Many of them have the feature of trying to show that if we acknowledge the reality of human beings as real persons or rational agents, then a condition of this understanding is that we accord them a certain status of making claims on our own actions.[4] One line of thought which I have always found very attractive is that of John Mackie who argued, by a method of elimination, that if we reject a duty based ethic as rule worship and a goal based ethic like utilitarianism as sacrificing individuals to the greater common good, then we are left with the idea that each individual has a status which needs to be respected i.e. a basic right.[5]

A feature of what I have said is this: we can think of a global ethic as an ethic supported by many ethical approaches including human rights thinking; likewise we can think of human rights thinking as itself an approach which can be supported for a number different reasons, intellectual, spiritual, secular and religious. With this framework in mind we can now ask how Quaker thinking about 'that of God' will fit in.

Clearly the idea of that of God in everyone is essentially a global ethic. It is the global ethic of an individual thinking about the status of all human beings. Whilst Quakers do not usually use the language of global ethics, it is clear that its central ethical/theological claim is a claim about all human beings, not just members of our own community, and that answering that of God is a matter of accepting responsibility across borders. On the other hand we have to be clear that our way of stating and understanding the basis of a global ethic is neither universally nor widely shared, and it would be unreasonable to suppose that more than a small minority of human beings will come to accept that way of understanding it.

Even if Quakers became great proselytisers – which I hope we will not do as that would undermine part of what makes us Quakers – it would be unrealistic to suppose that the majority of people would come to accept it. But given my framework, this should not be a matter for dismay, since we may be able to accept that we have *our* reasons for supporting shared values which others for *their* reasons share too.

Thus the first thing we can say is that Quakers, in having a global ethic, have reason to support human rights thinking of other people to the extent that this human rights thinking leads to endorsement of broadly the same global values – and this will be so even if some Quakers have their theoretical reasons for not wanting to say themselves that all human beings have human rights. I will come on to why Quakers might have reservations about this in a moment. On the other hand many Quakers may actually feel that the claim that we have that of God in everyone is in fact another way of saying that all human beings do have certain basic rights as human beings; so for them they can endorse the general idea that there are human rights, but accept that they have their reasons whilst many other people have many other reasons, both secular and theological, for saying that we have human rights.

From my own point of view, the second approach seems reasonable in that I do not think that the idea of human rights is inconsistent with a religious understanding of them, and as the other chapters indicate, one of the origins of human rights thinking was indeed theological (even though other strands of theological and religious tradition did not affirm this idea). But we must acknowledge that whilst we may support human rights thinking as supporting a global approach to ethics which Quakers also support, nevertheless there is something about the idea of human rights in its modern context, whatever its earlier religious origins, which jars with the Quaker conception of that of God in everyone.

It may be thought that the modern idea of human rights is too secular; that it has encouraged a rights culture in which people forget that they have obligations to respect other people's rights, but also as importantly, to exercise their rights in a responsible manner; that, even if the correlativity thesis that rights and duties always go together is accepted, this secular understanding of morality is quite different from the relationship which Quakers believe exists between individuals as one answering another because that other person has that of God in him or her. Although we *could* unpack the idea of answering that of God in another person in terms of that person's rights to the essential elements of his human well-being and another person's answering that of God as simply a duty to do so, it may be said that this relationship of 'answering' in Quaker understanding is poorly captured by the language of rights and duties.

Whether this is a reason for rejecting a human rights understanding of our own beliefs is a matter for discussion amongst Quakers, and I can well understand how Quakers will reasonably disagree on this matter. What I hope will not be so much a matter for disagreement is that Quakers can support human rights thinking generally, given our own starting points. And the corollary of this is that if two Quakers take two different views on the relationship between that of God and a human right, they can accept each other's differences and unite in what they can affirm and unite with everyone else committed to the human rights approach.

What I have said is not intended to iron out real differences that may remain in the way different people understand, interpret and apply their human rights thinking. But we may want to celebrate the areas of convergence, in the face of those who do not take a global approach seriously, particularly in their understanding of international relations and what states may legitimately do. To give you one concrete example: many years ago I was asked to talk on a panel about euthanasia, and I suggested that the right to life could be interpreted to include the right to choose not to live; and an ex-colleague of mine who was a Catholic deeply disagreed, claiming the right to life entailed the duty to preserve life in all circumstances. What was particularly poignant and sad for me was that for many years in the seventies he and I had work side-by-side campaigning for the third world, and had both used the same argument that the poor had a right to life. Clearly our different understandings of human rights led to a large area of convergence in regard to responding to world poverty, but in this very different area to do with euthanasia, we were pulling in different directions. I give this example partly because I suspect Quakers would be pulled in two directions too (and this suggests what I think is true, that we interpret that of God in various ways too).

I now turn back to the level of human rights thinking which has to do with national and international law, and the development of a human rights culture. It is I think even more obvious that, if these things help create the conditions in which that of God in everyone is more effectively answered, then Quakers ought to support the development of these things. And this would be so even for those Quakers who not only did not affirm their own beliefs in human rights terms, but also had a stop in their minds about human rights *ethical* thinking of others. We should consider a parallel which is rather striking. Jeremy Bentham, the classical utilitarian, was as many of you will know deeply opposed to what he saw as human rights thinking except for what was formulated in positive law – indeed he called it 'nonsense on stilts'.[6] Nevertheless he was an ardent campaigner for the reform of law and indeed the development of international law, which of course include the rights dimension, precisely because, given his utilitarian premises, he believed that the development of certain kinds of laws would indeed tend to the greater happiness of human beings.

This chapter has provided an analytic framework for thinking about the relationship between that of God talk and human rights talk, indicating a number different positions which Quakers could take up on this issue. In some respects it provides a substantial account of the issues, in other respects it provides an analytic tool for the consideration of other chapters in the book.

Notes

1. See especially the chapters by Bartlet, Cranmer and Hills.
2. A Utilitarian is generally concerned with assessing the rightness of acts in terms of their consequences, namely promoting the best balance of good over bad outcomes for all those affected: 'everyone is to count for one, none more than one'. See for instance the classical formulation by J.S. Mill (Mill, J S., 1861, *Utilitarianism*, in e.g. Warnock, M. (ed.), 1962, London: Fontana). A Kantian follows the thinking of Immanuel Kant and argues that there are basic duties not based on consequences which are applications of the 'categorical imperative'. One formulation of this which relates to our topic reads: 'So act that you treat humanity never merely as a means but as an end in itself'. (See for instance Kant, I., 1785, *Groundwork of the Metaphysics of Morals*, in e.g. Paton, H (tr.), 1949, *The Moral Law*, London: Hutcheson) These are common bases for the secular ethics of humanists, but they provide at least part of the basis for the ethical beliefs of many religious people as well.

3. See Dower for full development of this point (Dower, N., 1998/2007, *World Ethics – the New Agenda*, Edinburgh: Edinburgh University Press, chapter 6/5).
4. See e.g. Gewirth, A., 1987, *Reason and Morality*, Chicago IL: Chicago University Press; cf. Shue, H., 1996, *Basic Rights; Subsistence, Affluence and US Foreign Policy*, Princeton NJ: Princeton University Press.
5. See Mackie, J. L., 1984, 'Can there be a right-based morality?', in Waldron, J. (ed.), *Theories of Rights*, Oxford: Oxford University Press.
6. See Bentham, J., 1843, *Anarchical Fallacies*, in J. Bowring (ed.), *Works*, vol. 2., p. 523.

Human Rights: a Practical Approach

Roger Iredale

Abstract

Golding's novel *Lord of the Flies* demonstrates that human rights need to exist within a social framework of beliefs, procedures and other structures, without which the concept of rights is threatened. Hence, human rights are defined and arbitrated by human organisations, whether at an international, national or tribal level. In a complex and globalised world Quakers need to be able to discern what constitutes an infringement of a human right; to be able to do this accurately they need to be able to step outside the prevailing wisdom as offered by the media which frequently follow 'official' or government-led paths. Inherent contradictions within public statements by politicians and others indicate how reality is distorted to feed political positions. The half-truths and lies thus perpetrated undermine the democracy of our society, particularly in the absence of a Constitution. If we are not to lose our liberties, Quakers need to focus on repeated attacks on our freedoms and human rights.

William Golding's novel, *Lord of the Flies*, traces the steady descent by a group of stranded boys from a forced effort to recapture the rules, rights and order of the school world they have left behind them, to an ultimately dark and vicious survival of the most powerful at the expense of the weak and vulnerable.[1] The interruption of this steady decline into the brutality of tooth and claw by the *deus ex machina* appearance of a British naval unit symbolising the values of discipline, authority and order seems intended to show us how the wider world of 'civilisation' can moderate the inherent viciousness of human nature. When things get out of hand and human rights are trodden down, benign authority is the answer.

The novel naturally begs questions about the nature of human nature, the ability of human beings to exercise respect towards each other, and the precariousness of the 'rule of law' once it is removed from the context of an established human order of beliefs, traditions, procedures, hierarchies and levels of authority. In the real world human rights exist within a social context, be it that of a small isolated tribe or the United Nations. The rights are essentially defined by human organisation, whether family, tribe, republic or international order. In each case there has to be an assumed acceptance of certain norms by the majority, whether voluntary or coerced.

It becomes inevitable that in this scenario human rights will emerge as relative. Hence, in a particular context they may not include the right of slaves to be treated as free agents, or of women to have the right to education or the right not to be mutilated at birth. We are still working on the definition of the rights of children, which are widely regarded as differing from one society to another. Nor is the existence of a United Nations Organisation any guarantee that vulnerable groups will not be humiliated, dispossessed and murdered. Sudan, Burma and other places today illustrate this only too clearly.

At home the rights of mental illness sufferers are seriously threatened by political responses to media pressure based on a misunderstanding of the nature of illness and a panic and populist reaction to one or two high-profile cases of institutional neglect where the patient rather than the systemic failure of the treatment regime is blamed. In many instances it is religion itself that interferes with basic rights such as free speech (as in the case of Galileo), or equality of treatment (as in the case of women under the Taliban). In a globalised world, things are even more complicated as Christian zealots in the Mid West of the USA actively participate in the ethnic cleansing of Palestinians from their traditional lands.

The difficulty for Quakers, in a globalised world, is to discern which broadly accepted infringements of human rights exist in the first place, let alone how to address them. We assume that widespread opposition to the Slave Trade was based on a common perception that slavery was wrong and illegal, when in reality the realisation of its nature and inherent evil must have been incremental, reaching different elements of the white population only slowly. Early Quakers may well have believed that truly Christian conduct consisted of treating their slaves with kindness and humanity – but not freedom! It could even be argued that the underlying mentality of slavery continued up to and after the time of Martin Luther King, casting its shadow even today over the USA penal system, where hugely disproportionate numbers of convicts are black. In the present globalised world, modern human trafficking, which has been in operation for decades, is only now beginning to register as a serious problem, having been almost entirely invisible to most people until very recently.

For most people, recognition of systematic injustice and the avoidance of inherent bias in the presentation of 'facts' involves a major effort of will on the part of the individual to overcome the insidious slant imposed on the wider society by media and government. The journalist John Pilger has focused for well over a year on the slavish bias of journalists towards international news, as has a recent research report by the Universities of Manchester, Leeds and Liverpool.[2] Examples of this bias have become so familiar that they flit past our noses like midges on a summer evening: Syria and Iran are accused of supplying weapons to Hizbollah, while US and British exports of lethal munitions and arms are 'support for counter-terrorism'. Iran is accused of sending foreign fighters into Iraq by the very powers that have filled the country with huge alien armies. The British Prime Minister criticises Iran for undermining the elected Government of Iraq, while his government simultaneously works with the USA and Israel to demolish the democratically elected government in Palestine whose ministers are literally kidnapped without a murmur of protest from the international community and its people are starved for daring to support the 'wrong' kind of democracy. The distorting lens of media bias turns our world into the absurd fantasies of a house of mirrors.

Domestically it is difficult to assess whether Government is any more mendacious and scheming than it has been in the past. It took the Quakers to expose the scandal of British-run concentration camps in the Boer War, and we have only recently learned of the murder of Kenyan civilians during the Mau Mau era. World War I was the subject of a truly massive cover-up of the true conditions in the trenches.

Today we have better access than our forebears, and so the degree of subterfuge and sleight of hand is perhaps clearer sooner. My own files reveal a blatant lie by a minister to an MP, but at the level of simple deliberate misinformation of the public a good example is that of the identity card, sounding rather like a piece of paper with a picture on it, but concealing a massive and Orwellian database. Meanwhile a member of the Upper House seriously tells us that possession of the 'card' will not be obligatory 'because no one is obliged to take out a passport'!

The blatant lies, half-truths and teeming unipolar misdefinitions to which we are daily exposed not only undermine the moral health of our society, but blind us to the inherent contradictions on which many of us base our lives. If we are blind to or ignorant of the injustices and repressive measures that bear on ourselves, our fellow citizens and the rest of the world we cannot begin to formulate or exercise a human rights policy or approach. If the Society of Friends is to embrace a human rights ethic, whether that is distinctively 'Quaker' or a shared vision – ecumenical or whatever – its membership must first become acutely conscious of the issues confronting us. Before you can attack the Slave Trade you must become conscious of its existence and of its inherent evil.

It is regrettable that the establishment of individual or collective visions of human rights has to start from a profound mistrust of what we are told is the truth, or 'facts'. Nevertheless, scepticism has always been the primary tool of the scientist, and it can equally become the tool of the activist or the common citizen. Our first task is to be on our guard against the corrupting influence of misinformation. Wherever we can we need to speak out against bias and half truths.

But the second task is that of finding ways to uphold what few benign areas of authority exist: to support the weak, the vulnerable, and the put-upon. The United Nations, attacked, undermined and weakened by predatory nation-states, is worthy of support by whatever means. So are groups that aim to expose injustice and discrimination. Prejudice and distortion, whether it is provided via the slanted output of the BBC or by the privately owned and biased tabloids, requires rooted and systematic opposition. In a decentralised Society of Friends, groups need to be highly active in pointing out the realities to those less able to form independent critical judgements.

While activism – even mere verbal activism – may appear a nebulous and disorganised approach to a Quaker vision of human rights, it provides the basis for a decentralised and potentially widely readable body of information for other church members and the public at large. Monthly Meetings and other groups need to be encouraged to speak out on human rights issues, whether domestic or international, in ways that will reach others, either through letters to the press and MPs, or through vigils, posters and any other form of influence.

Any discussion of human rights must therefore accept both a wide range of definition of what constitutes a right and an acknowledgement that – even where there is consensus – human rights are commonly ignored and violated. To quote Michael Bartlet in this book, 'there is no right without a remedy'. The Soviet Union guaranteed considerable rights under its constitution, but disgruntled citizens had no remedy, and often perished for their beliefs.

Without a vision and a strategy, we risk ourselves becoming the victims of future human rights abuses. The lack of a constitution of the kind that characterises most other countries places all of us in great danger, as one 'inalienable' right after another is quietly and deftly removed by simple majority votes in the Commons, reluctantly but inexorably supported by the Upper House. A constitution does not of itself guarantee safety, as many countries have shown, but the absence of one almost guarantees future abuse. Quakers need to focus on the potential threat to freedom of speech and perhaps ultimately freedom to worship that are inherent in an unstable political system. If we do not wake up to this and other issues, we risk ourselves becoming the human rights victims of totalitarianism.

Notes

1. Golding, William, 1954, *Lord of the Flies*, Faber & Faber, London.
2. Robinson, Piers *et al.* 'Media Wars: News Performance and Media Management During the 2003 Iraq War', unpublished ESRC

research study no. RES-000-23-0551. Pilger, John, 'It never happened...' *New Statesman*, 30 July 2007, pp. 30-32; see also *ibid.,* 15 November, 2004, pp. 13-15; 11 April, 2005, pp. 21-22; 13 June, 2005, pp. 15-16; 17 October, 2005, pp. 30-31; 28 November 2005, p.24; 27 March, 2006, p.27; 24 April, 2006, pp. 18-19; 16 October, 2006, p.22; see also Iredale, Roger, 'BBC Israel Bias" (letter), *New Statesman*, 6 August, 2007, p. 6, and Halpin, David, 'Truth and the BBC' *ibid.*

Human Rights in Theory and Practice

Harvey Cox

Abstract

The first part of this paper makes some general observations on the development of the idea of human rights since the seventeenth century. It proposes a view of these as based on human life as an endowment of God or as a vessel for 'that of God'. It flows from this that the most basic human rights concern equality (of respect and treatment). They should be viewed as 'trumps' overriding other considerations such as politicians' views of what is in the public interest of the majority. The second part considers Northern Ireland since 1970 as a prime example of a case where the state came under pressures similar to those now posed by the threat of international terrorism. With examples, it argues that a vigilant regard for basic rights is key to securing a society free from resort to political violence.

Considering Human Rights – the 1650s and after

The three Abrahamic religions are each based upon combinations of text, tradition and institution. This is what renders them simultaneously universal and highly fissiparous. Ancestry for a wide range of currently held doctrines or concepts can be found within the past of each of the religions. The same holds true for more overtly secular traditions of thought. At least one 'Human Rights Reader' for students provides antecedents in the Bible, Plato's Republic, Aristotle, Cicero, St Augustine, Aquinas and de la

Casas.[1] Most of the texts cited, however, come from eras when nothing like the modern state existed, and at least some of these authors (e.g. Plato) have also more generally been cited as antecedents for doctrines inimical to human rights. Selective quotations is a game anyone can play. It is, I suppose, in itself harmless, if unconvincing. Quakers do it too.

Interestingly, Quakerism was born in a decade in which differing views of rights (e.g. of kingship) were at their most contentious, and blood (on a First World War scale, it is often forgotten) was shed over them. While Quakers in Britain today cherish as one of their few agreed principles that which holds that there is 'that of God' in everyone, along with those others, also dating from the C17th that, together, comprise the peace testimony, they are, again, rather highly selective in this. They have tended to preserve these elements from the founding era while rejecting much of the rest, including their Christocentric context (to a large extent). Furthermore, if 'that of God' in everyone *was* a central belief, it was hardly an activating one, in that the next two centuries of Quakerism were, with some exceptions, quietist. The peace testimony, as expressed in 1661, signified a withdrawal from political action, by a movement many of whose people had been in Cromwell's armies, after Quakers had ceased to believe in the imminence of Christ's kingdom. Thus it was more about an abjuring of politics than a springboard into it. From millenarianism, through pacifism, to quietism, in fact.[2] Quakers were pleading that they would play no part in armed opposition to the political status quo and therefore should be left alone to develop their spirituality (and their organisation) without hindrance.

James Nayler, in 1654, wrote that God 'made all men of one mould and one blood to dwell on the face of the earth'.[3] Nayler had a strong sense of social justice, like many at the ranter end of Quakerism. But by 1678 Robert Barclay had published attacks on ranter anarchy and theologised a return to a preoccupation with sin and adjustment to the state.[4]

Many Quaker ideas of the mid seventeenth century, including those of George Fox, were held in common with social radical movements in general; but only Quakerism survived. If any element of social thought survived the radical explosion of the mid seventeenth century it was a belief, not in human rights, but in human equality. Such a belief was potentially politically explosive, which was a powerful reason why it had to be tamed by enclosure within conventicle and meeting house walls. Quakerism, even if it went quietist for a very long time, nonetheless served as an ark, carrying a deposit of values derived from its faith and practices forward, where they re-emerged to public view in such activities as the campaign to abolish the slave trade, and the philanthropic and reformist movements of the nineteenth century.

The idea of rights in the mainstream of political discourse, however, came to be diverted away from the rights of kings, at least in the Anglo-American tradition, not towards human beings as equal, autonomous actors, but, via writers such as John Locke, towards the rights of individuals as owners of property. A political theory, it has been argued, of 'possessive individualism'. Thus, to take one example, the American Declaration of Independence (1776) roundly declares that 'we hold these truths to be self-evident, that all men are created equal, that they are endowed by their creator with certain inalienable Rights, that among these are life, liberty and the pursuit of happiness'. Fine sentiments, endorsed without apparent embarrassment, by an assembly including many slave owners.

The Founding Fathers indulged in this exercise in high-sounding rhetoric, so insouciant of the (to us) glaring hypocrisy involved in it, and America continued to mouth it, notwithstanding, for decades to come, for a fairly simple reason. The US was created by a coalition of territories and interests. It was not going to allow itself to founder on a philosophical abstraction. Two views on the Declaration, however, are possible. One, that the idea of a natural right is simply 'nonsense on stilts'. Bentham viewed the concept of a natural right as 'a son that never had a father', by which he meant an account of how rights come about. The idea of something being 'self-evident' is simply inadequate, not to say lazy. But the other viewpoint would see in the Declaration (for all its flaws in practical politics) some of the key elements in a theory of human rights – the idea of rights as 'endowed' by God, and the idea of equality as being at the root of the matter.

Arguably, despite the facts a) that much of the human rights tradition was forged *against* the opposition of institutionalised religion, holding as this tended to do, to versions of rights as belonging to God, as exclusively interpreted by the church, the mosque or the synagogue, and b) that the concept of human rights historically belongs more in a secular, humanist tradition; religion, because of its insistence on the transcendent, or, alternatively, the immanence of the sacred in man, can and should constitute a more secure home for human rights than a purely secular form of liberalism, at least in western countries. It ought almost to go without saying that the greatest violators of human rights, by any definition, have been the great totalitarian statisms based on militantly secular doctrines. But, following on from their eclipse, the apparent recent triumph of the liberal state has been succeeded by a situation in which it is driven by the exigencies of our times towards a set of tradeoffs of some human rights, of some people, against a concept of the general good which, of necessity, is defined predominantly by governments. In a situation of general alarm about 'security' the critiquing of state actions in this regard (as of the state's actions in regard to defence policy) needs a firm, principled rooting. The capacity of purely secular humanism to do this, not least because of its weak motivational ability, has to be doubted. Witness the virtual bankruptcy of ideas, in the last twenty years, of movements such as democratic socialism.

Hence I would argue for a revivification of the animating concepts of rights as a product of endowment by God, or of the sacredness of the human (the principle is the same, though ways of formulating it differ) and that of equality. In support of these I would refer to two writers, one a theologian-ethicist, the other a philosopher of law.

In his 'Ethics' drafted (though never finished) in Germany in 1940-3, Bonhoeffer argues that

> The existence of a natural right of the individual follows from the fact that it is God's will to create the individual and to endow him with eternal life.
>
> Since it is God's will that there should be human life on earth only in the form of bodily life, it follows that it is for the sake of the whole man that the body possesses the right to be preserved.[5]

He goes on to argue for rights as an extension of this – bodily life is rightly to be regarded as an end in itself, and hence its needs are extensions of this – shelter, play, fellowship, piety, natural joy, protection of innocence against arbitrary infringement of its liberty.

Bonhoeffer acknowledges, as any writer must, that, 'inherent in the natural itself' is conflict of rights, which 'demands the intervention of positive rights' which 'are to be both divine and secular.' At this point, his MS contains a pencil comment 'Must be developed later!' But it never was.

This does indeed raise the point, not only what *is* a right, in more specific terms than those discussed above, but which rights are, in situations of conflict of rights, to prevail over others. In his 'Taking Rights Seriously' (1991) Ronald Dworkin has produced one of the most significant philosophies of jurisprudence in recent times. He argues that no mechanical procedures exist for demonstrating what rights a particular individual has. There are always going to be hard cases. But, in his most noted formulation, Dworkin argues that we should see rights as 'trumps'. Rights become contentious where there is, at stake, a trade-off to be made between the interests of one or a few individuals against some concept of a more general societal interest. A 'right' is one that has the capacity to override interpretations of the collective general interest. Where society (which in practice means government and its agencies) takes 'tricks', rights are those things pertaining to individuals so basic as to warrant ring fencing against *any* view that their infringing would make the community as a whole better off. Trumps, in fact.[6]

Dostoyevsky, in '*The Brothers Karamazov*', gives a model, if characteristically extreme, example of what we might mean by human rights as trumps. His saintly, monkish character Alyosha is challenged by his brother to imagine that he could erect an edifice to make human beings happy, to give them peace and quiet at last, but that in order to do so it would be necessary to torture to death one tiny creature 'and on its unavenged tears to build that edifice.' Would he agree? 'No, I would not agree, Alyosha said quietly.'[7]

Although a certain number of human rights may be regarded as trumps under all circumstances – a right of freedom from torture or degrading treatment, a right to freedom from arbitrary imprisonment, a right to fair trial, other rights are not absolute and depend upon context. This really *is* self-evident. I do not have the liberty, as a right, to drive where and how I like, regardless. Nor, in an often-cited case, to shout 'fire' in a crowded venue – though I might have a civic duty to do so if there actually *was* a fire. The rights that are trumps, in Dworkin's view, cluster around not liberty, but equality. By this is implied rights to equal concern, respect and treatment, not necessarily as to outcomes (views differ legitimately on income distribution, for instance), but certainly as to procedures (e.g. before the law, or in matters of voting and representation). Dworkin's view, interestingly, accords better with the worldview of the C17th radicals, than more recent views prioritising liberty over equality.

The Northern Irish case – 1968-2000

A critical problem about the language of 'rights' today is that it can either become so widely used that it becomes a morass of philosophical conundrums (as in 'animal rights' or 'rights of the unborn') or, since rights are couched in laws, it can become excessively legalistic and impenetrable to all but lawyers. Hence, I suggest, the value of examining human rights in the context of actual political experience.

Since the turn of the millennium the UK, along with other western nations, has experienced pressures on its human rights protection mechanisms due to the development of real and perceived threats from militant political extremists. The most obvious example of this is the London bombings of 7th July 2005, which killed 52 people and maimed many more. But also the aborted attempt two weeks later, and other more recent cases. Northern Ireland, however, presents a prototype of the situation where the UK, as a liberal democratic state (however imperfect) already has had to respond to armed challenge from 'terrorists'. (The word is shorthand, needing a whole extra essay to demonstrate that it fits). All cases are unique; nevertheless some lessons may be drawn. Indeed, one of the latter-day functions of the Northern Irish armed conflict, and the drawn out peace process that has succeeded it, has been to provide lessons in the context of a setting quite characteristic of many contemporary armed conflicts; lessons both on what governments ought not to do, as well as how they might handle things properly. And, hopefully, perhaps, how to turn 'peace' from an aspiration to an activity.

Governments and societies faced with armed militants are likely to be dealing with grievances stemming from the operation of long, deep forces. Be that as it may, however, there is an immediate problem of developing an appropriate response to violence, which addresses the priority of protection of life. This should never crowd out the priority of addressing the causes of the alienation leading to the violence. The current US led 'war on terror' appears to give little weight to consideration of 'terror's' causes, as if it was *sui generis*. Nevertheless, governments have to act in the here and now.

In the Northern Irish case, the British Government in 1968-9 *did* move reasonably swiftly to address some of the most obvious causes of grievance; but they were also impelled by the immediate exigencies of crisis management in a situation of increasing communal polarisation accompanied by violence. In a divided society, one community's hopes were the fears of the other. While the initial taking to the streets concerned demands for certain specific 'civil rights' particularly about local government, the situation moved quite rapidly to a much more fundamental issue about the totality of relations between the two communities and, behind that, between Britain and Ireland. In handling the problem, successive British governments had to juggle with several different competing claims for priority; but to simplify, the principal dilemma was the balance between longer-term solution seeking and the need to handle what became an increasingly sophisticated campaign of violence. Could this violence (coming from two sides) be contained and stopped within the normal framework of a liberal-democratic state? The republican and loyalist paramilitaries were also citizens of the state, with substantial constituencies of support.

Northern Ireland was not Lincolnshire. Normal policing could not cope. A state that would not take special measures to respond to violence would find its stance perceived as weakness and its people turning increasingly to extreme politics and to warlords and mafias for protection. On the other hand, a state that took excessive measures, whether by its armed agents on the streets and in the countryside, or by modifications of normal expectations in respect of the substance and the administration of the law, would stir up the very mobilisation of political extremes that was at the core of its problem to begin with. One of the most noticeable features of internal conflicts is their capacity to self-fuel. Like brushwood fires, once a conflict has begun it feeds upon itself. The initial, fundamental grievance is never forgotten, but things move on and the handling of protest about the grievance becomes a new grievance, assimilating itself as a new chapter in a long-running book. In the classic Northern Irish case, the introduction of internment (Aug 1971) was the response to a long period of rising violence. Bloody Sunday (30-1-72) which killed 14 unarmed, albeit unruly, demonstrators in turn was the culmination of months of angry demonstrations, accompanied by violence, against internment. The subsequent judicial enquiry, under Lord Widgery, was hasty, superficial and biased, adding fresh insult to injury. These events served to funnel fresh recruits to the IRA (they could hardly cope with the numbers). Over thirty years later, the most expensive judicial enquiry in British history has still not laid the matter to rest.

Infringements of 'human rights' in Northern Ireland from 1968 onwards, by the state, tended to take two forms. Firstly, modifications of normal judicial processes (as they might operate in Lincolnshire) – internment without trial, the use of the Diplock (no jury) courts, the use of 'supergrass' evidence and the miscarriages of justice, involving police misconduct, in several high-profile cases in England (e.g. Birmingham Six). Secondly, abuse of emergency powers by security forces – inhuman and degrading treatment of people arrested under anti-terrorist legislation, shootings into crowds, as on Bloody Sunday already mentioned, and various 'shoot to kill' incidents. A particular feature here was the blurring of what should have been a clear distinction between security forces and 'loyalists', whose actions have been described as 'pro-state terrorism'. Another was the extreme reluctance to allow prompt and transparent investigation of incidents.

As illustration, we may cite two important 'incidents' which became very long running sores. In late 1982, seven men were shot dead by the police in three successive incidents in North Armagh. Five were completely unarmed; two others had been in a hayshed with three old, pre-war rifles. It was clear that the police deliberately misled investigators and ultimately the courts, in order to protect their procedures. In 1984 John Stalker of Greater Manchester Police was called in, after a public furore, to investigate. But in 1986 he was forced off, accused of 'improprieties,' and impelled to resign from the police – all in the interests of keeping the whole truth away from public revelation. The second 'incident' was the murder, in February 1989, of Patrick Finucane, a solicitor who had worked extensively for republicans. The killers were loyalist paramilitaries, but the weapon had come from the Holywood army base. Subsequent investigations made it clear that collusion between loyalists and security forces had taken place. A similar murder, also of a solicitor, Rosemary Nelson, took place some time later. More recently, in January 2007 the Northern Ireland Ombudsman, Nuala O'Loan, confirmed that collusion had taken place over twelve years between the police Special Branch and loyalist paramilitaries in North Belfast, resulting in at least ten deaths. Her report uncovered a culture of cover-ups, falsification of notes, destruction of evidence.

These were, simply, inexcusable abuses of police powers aimed at the removal of awkward individuals. But the boundary between an emergency measure and a human rights abuse is, in the nature of things, not always as clear-cut. Fair trial is a basic human right, but trial by jury is only a commonly accepted means to this end. Arguably the Diplock (no jury) courts provided better justice, in that juries do not have to give reasons for their decisions, whereas Diplock judges did, and these were subject to review. The problem here is more one of expectations. In the British and Irish political culture, the human right to fair trial has long been seen as *meaning* trial by a jury of ordinary citizens. In Northern Ireland, the departure from this in 1972 was seen by nationalists, and by many independent commentators, as an abuse of human rights. The case for the no-jury trials was not that strong; defects in the system such as intimidation of jurors, or the risk of perverse acquittals, was a problem indeed, but not so major a problem that alternative means of addressing it could not be found.

We need to bear powerfully in mind the pressures produced by the state's principal antagonists. These were determined, extremely well financed and armed, and no liberal democrats. Gerry Adams once said, quoting an old Irish adage, that 'he who is not strong had best be cunning.' His organisation undoubtedly was. In a famous phrase, Sinn Fein's Danny Morrison talked of taking power in Ireland with the ballot box in one hand and the armalite in the other. Someone rephrased this to run 'with the European Convention of Human Rights in one hand and the armalite in the other'. In large part Northern Ireland was the reason why Britain incurred the censure of Amnesty International[8] and was taken to the European Court of Justice more times over the last thirty years than any other subscribing state. In fact, of course, the Convention, and the British 1998 Act, incorporating it, does acknowledge the problem presented by terrorism and other emergencies by allowing for derogations. A state which chooses to be neutral between the fire raiser and the fire goes, and may deserve to go, the way of Weimar Germany. The problem however is whether the state, in its role as fire brigade, is really dowsing the fire or adding fuel to the flames.

Essential to the answer however, must be the holding of basic human rights as trumps. These should never be seen simply as only one set of factors in a Benthamite analysis favouring the greatest happiness of the greatest number. On the contrary, two things need to be said. One, as Dworkin has said recently, 'it is dangerous gibberish to say that the public has a right to as much security as it can have; no-one has a right to security purchased through injustice'.[9] Two, hard experience, not least in Northern Ireland, has shown that a disregard for basic human rights, even allowing for extreme pressures, will make conflicts more intractable, not less, even where, on occasion, measures taken might serve to offer a short cut, out of some form of security problem or legal quandary. We need to be as forthright as we can in pointing out the longer-term risks latent in such measures. In effect protection of and respect for human rights needs to be seen in a positive light not only as the *essence* of the liberal state, that which makes it 'civilised', but as a *resource* of the state against terrorists, whereas state infringement of human rights should be seen broadly as offering them gifts. In a general culture of political equality and respect for human rights there is much greater likelihood that fewer people will resort to terrorism and that those who do will lack broad support. We *may* still need to allow for limited, transparent, strictly controlled, short term, derogations from 'normal' procedures, but these will stand a greater chance of being understood and accepted rather than recycled into inducements to further violence.[10]

Notes

1. Ishay, Micheline R. (ed.) 1977, *The Human Rights Reader.* Routledge.

2. Hill, Christopher, 1994, *The Experience of Defeat,* Faber, pp. 124-63.
3. Hill, Ch., 1975, *The World Turned Upside Down,* Penguin 1975, p. 248.
4. *Ibid,* p. 254. See all of ch.10.
5. Bonhoeffer, Dietrich, 1960, *Ethics.* SCM Press, pp. 110, 113.
6. Dworkin, Ronald, 1991, *Taking Rights Seriously,* Duckworth, and *Rights as Trumps* in Jeremy Waldron (ed.), 1994, *Theories of Rights.* Oxford. See also Ingram, Attracta, 1994, *A Political Theory of Rights.* Oxford.
7. Dostoyevsky, Fyodor, 2003, *The Brothers Karamazov,* Penguin, p. 321.
8. Amnesty International, *UK Human Rights Concerns*, June 1991.
9. *The Guardian,* 2006, May 24.
10. On a recent visit to Northern Ireland, a panel from the International Commission of Jurists met with a wide group of specialists and involved people as part of a world-wide study of the impact of terrorism and counter-terrorism. Points made to the panel about the Northern Ireland experience included the importance of careful scrutiny of exceptional powers given to security forces; of limiting these as much as possible; of inculcating a culture of respect for human rights within them; of full, transparent and speedy response to abuses by security forces, including investigation of suspicious deaths; and of the necessity to address the causes of terrorism. See *Fortnight* magazine, Jun/Jul 2006.

Quakers, Human Rights and the International Responsibility to Protect (R2P)[1]

Alan Pleydell

Abstract

In the light of the developing doctrine on an international Responsibility to Protect (R2P) the chapter will consider what obligations may exist to protect target groups within state borders from lethal attack by their own governments. It will be suggested that the responses will vary according to the public roles and positions of those attempting to answer as well as according to the range of ethical views they may espouse. The chapter will assess what are the practical implications of accepting such duties for Quakers' interpretation of our Peace Testimony and what contributions we might make to public debate.

The Human Right to Life

There are a mounting number of instruments of international law according a general right to life to human beings purely in virtue of their humanity and envisaging sanctions against those who threaten or deny it – hence it is a human right. These include:

Convention on the Prevention of Punishment of the Crime of Genocide (1948)
Universal Declaration of Human Rights (1948) (article 3) (though this is non-binding)

International Covenant on Civil and Political Rights (1966) (article 6, 4) (this renders upholding the right to life binding on all states and bans arbitrary execution)

Siracusa Principles on the Limitation and Derogation of Provisions in the International Covenant on Civil and Political Rights (1984)

Principles on the Effective Prevention and Investigation of Extra-legal, Arbitrary and Summary Executions (1989)

Rome Statute of the International Criminal Court (1998) (article 6, 7j)

– as well as the Geneva Conventions as they pertain to protection of civilians in time of war.[2]

Immediate Context: the Desire to prevent Genocide

Against the existence of all these rights on paper is the obvious and painfully embarrassing fact that no-one really knows any foolproof way of preventing or putting a stop to large-scale abuse and killing inside internationally recognised state borders, without further and potentially unlimited force imposed from outside to stop them. Despite various expectations of the onward march of civilisation in our globalised age, massive and deeply shocking violations to the right to life have been going on uninhibited a great deal in recent decades and in many countries. They could even be said to be escalating as a result of the increasing levels of forced intimacy brought on by the intertwined processes of growth and globalisation. Yet these themselves are an inescapable part of the expansive human process which has been going on since the first emergence of our uniquely adaptive and acquisitive species.

We know that mass rape, forced displacement, bombarding and butchering large numbers of undefended people alive where they sit are utterly wrong. But without the consent of the largest power-wielding perpetrators on the ground, often the legally recognised governments of the territory themselves, such as those of Sudan and Burma at the moment, no one knows how to stop them short of forcing their cessation. Forcing the cessation from outside by bombing and invasion to create a 'more level playing field', as in Bosnia in 1995 and Kosovo in 1999, which was actually achieved, might create the space for mutual climb-downs, negotiations and an eventual road to some minimal political accommodation, such as provisionally occurred there. But even those interventions, often thought successful in their own terms of clearly preventing further major mass killing in the short term, have left the situation unresolved, and possibly incapable of resolution after already many years of hugely costly further international investment and military presence. In political/social terms, at the time of writing both interlinked cases remain severely dysfunctional and threaten further rounds of internal violence as well as further contributions by the situations to broader international conflict, partly as a result of the return of Russia under Vladimir Putin to the big power league.

Bombing or invasion of Sudan or Burma or, not to mince words, waging wars against them, unlike the claimed-to-be tactically neat, and therefore comparatively justifiable, 'surgical' wars of relief of the Balkans, if seriously considered, would not be such short-term or clearly bounded operations rendered so by decisive superior American (and in the Kosovo case British) power. They would involve hugely greater military investments and hugely greater violence, with no prospect whatever of negotiating a way to a viable political future, so complex are the multiple tribal claims and shifting alliances. They would be bound to involve degrees of entanglement which might easily get as completely out of hand and unendingly destructive as those in Afghanistan and Iraq.

Alan Pleydell

'Never Again!' has been the rhetorical cry in case after case of these dreadful manifestations of state-internal violence we are considering. Yet case after case continues to occur without serious external opposition if the government in question is really determined to pursue its ends, often to prevent secession and break-up of the state (itself legal), by the murderous means it deems necessary. What is the problem? Governments were and are legally protected from interference in the territories under their control by outsiders by the doctrine of state sovereignty, and this remains in logical conflict with and in law arguably at least equal to the claims of human rights, even if the latter is far higher in ordinary morals and most understandings worldwide of religious obligation. When the chips are down which gives way? Frequently there is the profoundest desire to help from outside, which tends to lead on to a belief in the potential benefit of deploying armed forces under the United Nations or some UN-authorised regional international bodies such as the African Union to stop abuse or prevent escalation. And they may, as I believe is possible, indeed be a help in the short term, in Hobbes' phrase, 'taking the world as it is'; and there is so much also that can go disastrously wrong, not only for the interveners themselves, but those they are supposed to be helping.

The International Responsibility to Protect

The evolving doctrine of R2P is an attempt, as yet not fully tested, to provide a doctrinal basis for the 'international community' to gain theoretical and practical purchase on these situations, by means of an evolving modification of the received doctrine of state sovereignty, such that failure of a country to accept and act on its responsibility to protect the lives of large parts of its own population will result eventually and as a last resort, in a forced response, with or without the consent of the government in question, after all other measures of prevention or dissuasion have been exhausted. There are three acknowledged parts to this responsibility – to Prevent, React and Rebuild. In the most recent formulations, particularly from the UN General Assembly in 2005,[3] the preventive and reactive responsibilities to protect lie first with the government of the state in question, and the emphasis is increasingly preventive. Both, however, particularly if the government itself is a or even the major perpetrator, necessarily invoke the interest and responsibility of the outside world, where the government is either unable or unwilling to react. The last resort issue, of not only external diplomatic suasion and pressure but also the contemplation and deployment of force, comes into play when there appears no way either to prevent or react from within and the killing continues apace. Some of the milestones in the development of this movement have been:

- The Canadian Government sponsored report of the International Commission on State Sovereignty (ICSS), December 2001[4] – the public origin of the phrase 'Responsibility to Protect'
- Appointment of a Special Advisor to the UN Secretary General on Prevention of Genocide, July 2004
- Report of the High, Level Panel on Threats, Challenges and Change, December 2004
- In Larger Freedom – Kofi Annan, UN Secretariat, March 2005 – response to the High Level Panel
- Outcome document of the UN World Summit, September 2005 – unanimous endorsement of the principles of R2P by all the member states the UN General Assembly
- UN Security Council Resolution 1769 unanimously adopted, 31 July 2007[5] – authorisation of a 26,000 strong UN/African Union force in Darfur (augmenting the under-equipped African Union force of 7,000).

As envisaged, external interventions under R2P vary from good offices proffered and accepted or welcomed voluntarily at the 'soft' end, through more or less smart economic sanctions, through military deployment to assist ceasefire, disarmament, stand-down, reintegration and rebuilding – all with the consent of the government in question,[6] right through to full-scale bombing or invasion in the face of its persistent intransigence at the fully 'hard' end, although these options would have to be argued for in detail as claimed to be necessitated by any case.

Many of R2P's advocates, including one of its principal advocates Gareth Evans,[7] say that its whole point is to avert the need for military intervention by creating and holding open the space for developing preventive options and getting them to stick, a line which I have argued at length myself on the analogy of the use of preventive training, education and social work to prevent child abuse in families under the umbrella of the ultimate forceful sanction of the law which have developed in the last decades. The whole gamble here lies in believing that a culture change can be effected by both having the threat of coercion available but keeping it in abeyance and in the background in most cases and most of the time. The idea is by degrees to evolve to the 'win-win' situation of both keeping the family, or state, together as well as the victims no further molested or at least alive, creating a holding situation whilst the primary abusers (and there are often many in the field besides the government itself) are gradually converted to milder ways.

Keeping things towards the preventive end of the range of options apparently works to a remarkable degree in cases of child abuse, to the extent of the culture change being tangible if in many places still its early stages. Cruelty and violence are on average far less evident in the majority of, let us say, western European families than they used to be. However that may be, success in this arena depends on being prepared to intervene coercively in the most extreme cases and where all else has failed, in so doing at least temporarily breaking up the family even in the midst of a growing general norm and practice of gentler behaviour in previously violent families. The prevention of child murder may simply require the forceful removal and incapacitation of the (often but not always male) violent parent from the scene for as long as he remains an active danger. And even Quakers, though not particularly liking it, may see this as the acceptable 'lesser evil' for the time being, pending longer-term cultural change. My guess would be we made a similar practical choice, two hundred years ago in relation to the abolition of the slave trade, though no more did it actually resolve the dilemma then than now.[8]

This may be where the analogy with state-internal population abuse in the current international scene breaks down. Here, the more intransigent the abusing government and the more it raises the stakes by further abuse, the greater will be the temptation to resort to 'the last resort', and bomb or invade, or at least threaten to, but therein lies the trap. That option may be so horrendous in its consequences as to be even worse and be known to be so on all sides. This is precisely the situation in which the abusers may call the bluff of the interveners and persist with their abuse. For the structure to work in the remedial way envisaged, the 'soft' option needs to kept open and available by the would-be helpful and diplomatic intervener, but such an intervener cannot remain credible in any sort of protection role in the face of the abuser continuing to escalate his use of atrocity to gain his ends.[9] The issue is then forced. The option then apparently becomes to bomb or invade on the one hand, or on the other to withdraw in shame, allowing the abuse to continue.

The abuser may be so entrenched and permanent a part of the scene just not to be removable at all and the hope of getting him to change his spots through consent may in practical terms be a forlorn one in any immediately foreseeable future. And the abused may not be practically rescuable either, except by keeping open 'humanitarian corridors' (say to refugee camps in Darfur), with the qualified and easily withdrawn consent of the abuser continuing only so long as it does not disrupt his major strategy of fatally weakening his perceived or real opponents (by continuing to destroy villages – honestly or otherwise seen as the source of rebellious activity). Where the abuser has the whip hand and intends to keep using it, the soft intervener has nowhere to go except either to comply with such strictures, winding up being or being seen as the abuser's dupe in furthering his strategy, or withdrawing or calling in international 'hard' power to level the field and support her/his efforts, escalating to armed intervention, unless the abuser can be induced to relent by appeal.

In short, the unresolved and perhaps unnresolvable dilemmas of these situations exist within the R2P doctrine itself and if this is so, it may not have taken us much further forward. At the soft end, everything depends on the gamble paying off – both the intervention remaining benign and under consent, and the molester gradually relenting and softening. If any of these conditions are not met, the intervener either has to withdraw in sorrow and shame or to get involved in support from international coercion which may result in larger scale and more prolonged violence and suffering on the part of many more innocent people. But that is true at the hard end too. Deciding much earlier to intervene forcefully to stop an abuse, may have a higher chance of succeeding in prevention in the short run and in some cases (perhaps concerted action from a united Europe could have prevented the beginning of the Yugoslav meltdown in 1991, though no such unity was in fact to be had), but there is no guarantee against the reverse result in many more cases of entering endlessly into a quagmire, both immoral and horrific.

Who supports R2P in principle?

In theory, the supporters include all the member states of the UN, all the NGOs and citizens' groups who have made public statements in its favour, including prominently Amnesty International, Oxfam International, International Crisis Group,[10] the World Federalist Movement, and indeed the World Council of Churches. But amongst governments at least, since no-one wants to see meddling in their own back yard, there will always be arguments, some of them very good or at least plausible ones, as to why the principles do not apply in one's own case, either from the point of view of contributing forces or of having one's country 'interfered' in, however 'helpfully'. This makes the issue not so different from consideration of many other human rights questions. It turns out that the universalisation of standards is fine so long as it is primarily about the civilisation of other places! Even though the 26,000 UN/AU troops may have been authorised for Darfur, it is a long way to seeing their both effective and comparatively harmless deployment. That depends on the active will of contributing governments (who will mostly be looking at one another to see how little they can get away with contributing – aware both of the costs and the prospect of getting inextricably bogged down), and the consent of the Sudanese government (since its sovereignty is upheld in the relevant resolution even though it is a major sponsor and perpetrator of the killings).

What about Quakers?

There have been a number of internal Quaker discussions of the difficulties and challenges raised by the issues of genocide prevention and R2P, with no very clear result – which is to be expected given the range of attitudes present amongst Quakers on most issues. At the formal/organisational level, however, the nearest we have got to an expression of sympathy with R2P principles is to unite with the peaceful parts, the preventive and rebuilding parts, but not with the doctrine as a whole, because, however much reduced in emphasis, it relies in the 'reactive' part on the forceful 'last resort', which clashes with our public perception as being pacifists, or at least as being those who attach great importance to always pursuing peace by peaceful means. But owing to its structure, you cannot unite with some of the parts without uniting with the whole. R2P requires and logically relies on support for all its parts to work. The Quaker sticking point has been expressed like this: 'Our means are the ends in the making', hence we ought not to do or collude with anything potentially violent.

In the end I believe that consistency is not to be had. We either stand aside from having any truck with intervention of any form which may turn violent (on 'our' side) if it is to be sustained and, in some sense, even if we are appalled, by our inaction we practically acquiesce in the continuation and escalation of mass murder uninterrupted.

Or alternatively, we give some form or support, however qualified, to forceful interventions which may or may not in fact relieve the suffering and which may or may not have widespread and long-lasting bloody consequences greater than the original violence. Hoping to avoid those consequences by facing down bloody opponents with the threat of unacceptably dire consequences to their own survival, though it might work (on the same logical basis as all deterrence), is just as much an insecure gamble, morally as well as factually, as the insecure gamble of hoping to court the abuser's goodwill whilst he persists in destruction . It also involves the real and morally unacceptable risk that it both will not work and involve our involvement, lock, stock and barrel, in the militarisation that backs the threat with all of its longer and wider consequences.

Quakers strive for peace and are 'pacifists'. Actually we espouse a 'peace testimony' which is expressed in various verbal forms in our history as well as in a variety of practical commitments. This is how we are publicly known. At the same time some of us and maybe most of us struggle with dilemmas provoked by our pacifist stance and some find it difficult to describe ourselves consistently as pacifists, even if we do indeed strive for peace.[11] No one so far as I know has ever produced an intellectual defence of pacifism, if that means absolute abstention from force or involvement with it, which is morally watertight. There is always more than some sense of unpalatability when its implications are taken to their logical conclusions and there is no escape from this – at least if we assume that we intend our arguments to apply to others as well as ourselves. In contemporary conditions, to put it in brutal terms, it means that the absolutely undefended will go on being undefended and therefore dismembered and slaughtered at will by their oppressors in very large numbers, short of an unforced change of heart on the part of those who have the upper hand over them and are already in mid-killing spree. And that seems to imply that we hold this to be morally preferable to adopting any means which might involve the use of force, even if conditionally. If we say our arguments are only for ourselves, why should anyone listen to us, and by what token do we exempt ourselves from ordinary public discourse and responsibilities? If we speak, surely we seek to persuade. As moral philosophers and students of political theory know only too well, if we take absolute positions on any practical question, it will ultimately lead us not only into absurdities (on paper) but also potentially to colluding with or not opposing horrors in any practical way – whichever side we take.

If we find some sort of necessity in going along with some defined form of military intervention or at least interposition in order to stop or prevent bloodbaths, then we share in the responsibility for the intervention ushering in even worse chaos and bloodshed. ... But if we oppose such interventions in all cases and on principle, we may have to recognise that this position inherently leaves those barely surviving and under direct lethal attack in incomparably worse conditions than ourselves with neither respite, nor escape, nor defence.

Do we believe that governments face the same schedule of imperatives and choices as private citizens – or do we allow that they have duties over and above ours? And is allowing them the use of coercive potential which hopefully won't but might turn bloody part of that? If we are talking about only what we would or do choose ourselves, does that not simply mean that we are wrapping ourselves in the luxury of pretending to be merely private citizens, actually living in comparatively safe and luxurious circumstances, without any consideration of our civic duties, through what our governments may or may not do, to other people around the world who are acutely in need of rescue and will carry on being slaughtered otherwise?

If we hold out for the pacifist position, I would suppose that we have to supply a credible account of what not only we, but everyone else, should do instead, not only private citizens, but governments, and show that even if it is not more likely to achieve the rescue of the tens of thousands already in direct and dire peril than any proposed deployment of force, at least by practical example we are making some contribution to rendering such situations less likely in the future, even if it only by attempting to clarify the arguments.

Is dissuasion with force (deterrence) by governments or public authorities part of what we sometimes allow? If it is, in what sense can we claim our stance to be essentially different from that of any private citizen who allows government to do on behalf of public safety what s/he does not allow to him or herself? If it is not, are we consistent in that or do we have some sort of rules of thumb which allow us to discriminate with any clarity between those forms of deterrence that we allow and those that we frown on?[12]

Quakers most of the time, maybe not always very consciously, recognise that we are systematically implicated and involved in a society which precisely relies on the conditional potential for the deployment of force in the very fact of having police who rely on superior force to effect arrests and forms of coercive custody to sustain the practical containment and incapacitation of those in our midst bent on violent destruction. As far as I know, we do not object to the deployment of police in public protection even knowing that the use of superior force inherently carries the risk of bloodshed, with or without guns. And although we may seek to ameliorate the conditions of custody in a hundred ways, I am not aware that we seriously argue for its abolition. If we are not anarchists, we expect to live in and be implicated in some sort of rule of law involving these restrictions. We may prefer this to be backed mainly by consent and strive for its increase, but we do not have a panacea to deal or contend with the widespread presence around us of non-consent to self-restraint and therefore the actual use of violence on the streets and we should not pretend to, unless we ourselves trust that we would be able to talk down an armed attacker unassisted by any potential forceful back-up. We hope that these situations can be managed without bloodshed and that we, like others, may or may not have various kinds of insight or experience which might contribute to diminishing the risk, but the risk cannot be eliminated in all cases. Because of this inextricable involvement in society and in mankind, to recall John Donne, it is difficult for us to purport to stand aside from allowing forceful protection from outside in the international case of forceful protection from violent abuse within other states, whilst knowing that we rely every day of our lives on equivalent protections.

My personal view is that if we do attempt to stand aside in this way, to uphold a kind of exemption for ourselves even in the knowledge of our systematic implications in all kinds of systems which involve the use or threat of force in the world we actually inhabit, then at least we have to supply in our daily commitments and actions some practical compensation for the succour that we may seem at least implicitly to deny to others.

First, we should never be involved in the condemnation of those who see things differently – including the condemnation of their acts – if we cannot sustain our objection consistently. The best we can do is argue for a space for our conscience-guided choice and not deny the same to others because we say their position involves acquiescence in violence, when if we are honest and take all factors in the round into consideration, we know very well that our position too may involve our own acquiescence in violence in different but morally or spiritually no less questionable ways.

Secondly, as Quakers, we should not pretend to have the answers or to have a unified view, nor be shy to display in public the full range of different opinions which exist amongst us on these questions. They perplex anyone of integrity and conscience who tries to think the issues through, and not just pacifists or Quakers. The complexity of actual cases on the ground hugely complicates and confuses the moral as well as the practical issues of what to do on all sides.

To allow ourselves to be understood as publicly purporting to be in possession of a superior way which however we are unprepared to unfold in all of its details and implications for particular hard cases on the ground, invites our dismissal as holier than thou prigs. That judgement may in some cases ring true where we have not even begun to experience the true weight and awfulness of these dilemmas of ultimate questions in our own breasts. We may not have done so in any way comparable with the efforts of those who, even whilst admitting seeing some form of necessity for some use of force in these direst of circumstances, do so with true trepidation and full acceptance of their own responsibility, whatever the outcomes. It may be true that there are some who sit lightly to these questions – but they are probably equally distributed amongst supporters or deniers of forceful intervention to save lives.

What matters in the end is not what we say but what we do – where we pitch our tent and where we take our stand – in full knowledge of our ignorance, limited capacities and lack of foresight – what in other words we simply commit to, hoping for the best. That will depend not only on ultimate moral questions and our grasp of them, but on much more prosaic considerations of what we are capable of. In the current conditions of the world, not in an as yet unapproached utopia of the general disarmament of states, which may be absolutely desirable in the long run but not around the corner, I personally find myself still believing in the potential utility and necessity of UN authorised and supervised peacekeeping troops.

However they are absolutely no panacea, and there are a hundred things to go wrong, as already demonstrated in Kosovo and elsewhere. Even in the face of horrors which seemingly cry out for forced intervention like Sudan or Burma, they cannot be used in this way to force change from the outside without major risk of becoming a huge part of the problem rather than the solution. So in practice the cases of justified intervention may be rare indeed.

Finally, in illustration of this point, the writer on African security matters Alex de Waal has recently argued[13] that in a case as complex as that in Sudan, the impact of calls for forced military intervention in Darfur invoked under R2P, under the understanding that the continued outrageousness of government behaviour long ago left no further 'soft' option, has been severely to inhibit and curtail the seriousness of commitment and exploratory intellectual effort invested by the international community. What is limited is its attempt to obtain and guarantee a proper ceasefire that will stick in advance of any deployment of international troops who might have a chance of either holding the line once it is in place – or proceeding from there towards assistance in disarmament and further moves towards de-escalation and the establishment of some sort of normality. In the last two years the rebel forces have further fragmented into more factional infighting, and De Waal's very cogent argument is that short of at least the skeleton of an agreement under broad principles, credibly committed to by all parties simultaneously, and with some practical guarantees made by them on the ground, the deployment of international peacekeepers will be completely foolhardy. They cannot possibly force a cessation of fighting themselves or attempt to disarm any of the belligerents against their will without immediately being inextricably dragged into the fight as belligerents themselves, which can only complicate and worsen the situation and render their position untenable. The African Union forces have already come under attack from various rebel factions. Even an augmented AU/UN force of 22,000 plus, if mustered and deployed and not endlessly obstructed and delayed by Khartoum as part of a cynical cat and mouse game, cannot force a peace in the absence of consent, or if it tries cannot avoid being identified as for some and against others or having to hold the ring for the long haul.

As De Waal says, the problem with R2P is that in the Darfur case it has fixed attention on attacking the Khartoum government or seeking to replace it by some sort of forced regime change in order to relieve the burden on its victims when in fact this is not obtainable by such means. The primary power holders are going to remain around in some potent form or other even if they are dislodged by elections or some other force. Much energy he says has been wasted on an inadequate concept, which when push comes to shove inevitably points to forced regime change. In fact the real problem lies with an insufficient concentration on the complexities of the politics and the need to strike a deal amongst all the factions on the ground in the end no matter how nasty they are and however difficult it is, since all will remain in play whatever happens.

However much we may be appalled by the recognition of it, much the same logic applies to the situation in Burma. No-one has a credible plan for how to reverse the situation militarily from outside which has the remotest chance either of being tried, or if tried coming off without even worse destruction and suffering.[14] In the end, in most of these cases of state-internal abuse, the prospect of any lasting relief comes down to the capacity of people in the territory themselves to find their way out of the complex morass that they have unwittingly fallen into, and that applies equally to perceived or actual perpetrators and victims, who somehow or other in the end have to find their way to future co-existence. That does not prevent our striving by might and main to discover ways to help genuinely. Often there will be not even that possibility – but that does not logically usher in the thought that an invasion or air campaign with unthought-through consequences can possibly make things better for those suffering most.

Notes

1. The views expressed in this piece are offered in a personal capacity.
2. Source: http://www.hrea.org/learn/guides/life.html.
3. See below.
4. Ottawa, International Development Research Centre, December 2001.
5. It invokes Chapter 7 of the UN Charter to authorize the use of force to protect civilians, maintains the sovereignty of the Government of Sudan, but reaffirms the 2005 Outcome Document on the responsibility to protect populations from genocide, war crimes, ethnic cleansing and crimes against humanity. (seehttp://www.hrea.org/learn/guides/life.html).
6. The history of the UN and the 'international community's' involvement in the Balkans in the 1990s is littered with the contradictions of this position, up to and including the UN's self-protective withdrawals from Rwanda and Srebrenica.
7. Former Australian Foreign Minister, one of the original 2001 R2P authors and President of the International Crisis Group, ICG.
8. Quakers certainly were major leaders in the abolition movement. They must then have been faced with the dilemma, once abolition was enacted, whether to approve of its enforcement. Their principles must have brought them to a fork in the road. They wanted abolition to succeed (hence backing the enforcement to backing the law

– the slavers were not going to give up without a fight), but they did not want to compromise their non-violence. The only way to have one's cake and eat it in such circumstances would be to refuse to participate directly. In logic there is no having your cake and eating it. My guess is that in conscience they chose one option or the other and swallowed hard, the majority going for consent to enforcement.
9. This is what happened in September 2007 in Burma, and basically for the moment at any rate, despite the visit of a UN envoy, the rest of the world has backed off whilst the killing has continued apace.
10. Gareth Evans, its president and former Australian Foreign Minister, may be said to be the continuing prime mover behind R2P as an organising concept.
11. The late Peter Brock, pacifist, conscientious objector and foremost historian of pacifism and author, amongst many other books and papers on pacifism, of *The Varieties of Quaker Pacifism: A Survey from Antiquity to the Outset of the Twentieth Century* (1998, Syracuse, NY: Syracuse University Press), was all too deeply aware of the logical and moral difficulties present within all forms of pacifism. It appears not to have put him off his stance. My guess would be that he would say that similar moral and logical difficulties attend all stances towards war and peace, pacifist or not. He may not have said this but we are all faced with the riddles, paradoxes and dilemmas provoked by Jesus's saying 'render under Caesar that which is Caesar's and unto God that which is God's' and at the end of the day for practical purposes, like everyone who is morally alive and sensitive to the reality of dilemmas, which means most people, we find ourselves pitching our tent where we feel we must, not in any conviction that there is any final adequacy to the stance taken. We are all equally under ultimate or divine judgement in this respect as well as under the scrutiny of our peers, be they contemporaries or those who come after – subject to the judgement of 'history' – which may or may not amount to the same thing.
12. All deterrents, to be credible, have to be backed by the intention to follow through with the conditional threat in actuality when the deterrer's bluff is called. The alternative position, as for the UN forces in Rwanda in Srebrenica, or rather for their superior commanders not in the field was not only to retreat in shame but to allow, almost to invite, the massacre of those they were supposed to protect.

13. De Waal, A., 2007, 'Darfur and the failure of the responsibility to protect', *International Affairs*, Chatham House, vol. 83, no. 6, November 2007, pp. 1039-54.
14. There is always an entirely valid riposte to the claim that surely things can get no worse than they are already being allowed to become; unfortunately, yes they certainly can.

International Aspects of Quaker Human Rights Work

Judith Baker

Abstract

The Universal Declaration of Human Rights has sometimes been criticised as a 'western' document. This paper will examine the Quaker experience of this, both at project level and at the UN. It will discuss whether Quaker work to interpret these rights for today's world should take into account different perspectives from differing religions and cultures. Quakers have brought several unpopular positions into the UN arena and obtained recognition for them. For example, the right to conscientious objection to military service, based on the right to freedom of conscience and religion. Former UN Secretary General Kofi Annan is reported to have said that it was not the people of the world who criticised currently recognised international standards of human treatment, only their governments.

The moral norms lying behind the UN's Universal Declaration of Human Rights seem to most in the UK to be relatively straightforward. It is challenging, therefore, to meet people who have a totally different view. For example, 'fairness': for me, 'fairness' might mean that a taxi has a meter and I pay the price on the meter. To the taxi driver in Egypt where I worked for two years the price on the meter is unfair, he switches it off. To him, 'fair' is that the rich foreigner pays more per minute or mile than a poor local woman. For many people in poorer countries in particular it is wrong to consider as equally important, for example, the right of an individual not to be tortured with the right of a whole population to have access to clean water. Tolerance, similarly, can be interpreted differently in different cultures: the idea that one might disagree strongly with another's opinions but defend absolutely his or her right to hold such opinions is not a common one, in some cultures this interpretation of tolerance may equate more to stupidity than virtue.

It is comparatively easy to be tolerant of anything except intolerance, but a person a westerner might perceive as intolerant is in their own eyes defending Truth or Honour or some other deeply held value. Collective identity is also stronger in some other cultures, an individual life being for many not nearly as important as we consider it in the west, but total identity with family, clan, tribe or nation is far stronger and almost beyond our western comprehension. In the UN system government representatives from all over the world meet and talk, together with almost as diverse non-governmental organisations (NGOs) keeping a watch over their work and feeding in information and ideas. The UN's greatest difficulty is how people and governments holding all these diverse notions of what is right can work together and improve that which needs to change. It would seem that this is one of the reasons progress is so slow, and to many outside the system it can seem as if diplomats do nothing but agree to meet again. Intergovernmental and expert human rights discussions are held in several different UN bodies, the 1948 Universal Declaration of Human Rights has been joined by various subsequent UN Covenants, Declarations, Protocols and Conventions, all 'promoting and protecting human rights'.

Friends World Committee for Consultation (FWCC) accredited the Quaker United Nations Offices (QUNO) in Geneva and New York in 1948 to work on behalf of worldwide Friends to support the UN in its efforts to abolish war and promote peaceful resolution of conflicts, human rights, economic justice and good governance.

International Aspects of Quaker Human Rights Work

Winston Churchill is reported to have said the UN was set up, not to get us into heaven, but to save us from hell, and perhaps with this in mind, Quakers have been there ever since, slowly and quietly putting into action our belief in the equality of all people and the value of each human life. Using our experience from social reform and justice work in the UK, practical peacebuilding work in conflict and post conflict situations and from Friends worldwide, the links are made amongst local, national and international aspects of Quaker witness. Perspectives from different religions and cultures inform the work; however any alteration in Quaker principles in response to some seeing the standards as 'western' or Judeo-Christian would suit only the perpetrators and not the victims of human rights violations. Former UN Secretary General Kofi Annan (a Ghanaian) is reported to have said that it was not the people of the world who criticised currently recognised international standards of human treatment, only their governments.

QUNO's Human Rights and Refugees programme has particular reference to the interface between human rights and armed conflict. The questions of the rights of indigenous peoples, gender, and violence against children are included in all programme areas. With its limited resources, QUNO cannot work on every human right, nor even on every human right of particular concern to Quakers. Often discernment leads to prioritising work on areas which require timely intervention, are not being addressed by others, or would benefit from the unique way in which Quakers work. The specific topics which form QUNO's current (2007) priorities are: child soldiers; protection of refugees; conscientious objection to military service; women in prison and children of imprisoned mothers; rights of indigenous peoples and the move from the UN Commission on Human Rights to the new Human Rights Council.

QUNO organises informal, off-the-record meetings to promote and enhance dialogue, networking and the building of relationships on human rights and refugee issues between government representatives across the regional groups of the UN, amongst the key non-governmental organisations and across the government, NGO, UN secretariat and independent expert spectrum. Such meetings encourage a greater understanding of why there are disagreements and provide an opportunity to challenge assumptions between those who would not otherwise have the chance to talk openly. Participants may try to find common ground or to explore difficult, controversial or sensitive issues.

London Yearly Meeting considered human rights in 1986. The Minute says in part, 'Above all we must take risks for God: look around us to the people who need help; listen to those who experience oppression; engage in the mutual process of liberation.' [Quaker work at the UN exists to ensure] 'that the standards and ideals of the Universal Declaration of Human Rights are attained, that the world does not slip backwards.'[1] This does not necessarily make us popular! Conscientious objection to military service was, for almost all governments initially, a very damaging and abhorrent concept. QUNO worked for decades to relate it to the right to freedom of thought, conscience and religion. The breakthrough came in 1986 with the government members of the UN Human Rights Commission agreeing that conscientious objection to military service is a legitimate exercise of that existing right. Since that decision, in November 2006, the right to conscientious objection to military service was recognised unequivocally by the Human Rights Committee, when deciding two cases from the Republic of Korea. The Committee held that the Korean Government had violated Article 18 of the Covenant on Civil and Political Rights (right to freedom of thought, conscience and religion) by failing to provide for conscientious objection. Interestingly, Quakers were not the first non-governmental organisation to bring this subject to the UN, and amongst the first governments to endorse it were Saudi Arabia and the Philippines,

International Aspects of Quaker Human Rights Work

not just the usual human rights champions such as the Netherlands and Austria.[2] Thus whilst being sensitive to the diverse moral and political heritage of the delegates from around the world, Quakers, working with others, persuaded the international community to include a Quaker principle in their interpretation of a 'human right', which now can help individuals in any country of the world.

Quaker Peace and Social Witness (QPSW) is a very small organisation. Over the years its role as catalyst and connector has enabled change, by working alongside others in slightly different ways to those of larger organisations necessarily driven by funding requirements.[3] Human rights forms a component of this primarily peacebuilding, overseas locally-based work. In South Asia QPSW has enabled a network of peace organisations from the whole region to come together, learning from each other and from QPSW too. During a nonviolence training workshop for the South Asian Peace Alliance (SAPA) run by QPSW in Nepal, INSEC, a local human rights and social justice group that worked with our Nepalese hosts, introduced a woman with whom they were working. She told of her desperation, a future raising children on her own after Nepalese government forces killed her husband. Another SAPA workshop participant, a young woman from Sri Lanka, helped to give hope and courage to this victim of human rights abuse by telling her own story of being raised by her mother alone, after the Tamil Tigers had killed her father.

In the former Yugoslav countries a QPSW peacebuilding programme runs many and varied support meetings, alternatives to violence trainings and dialogue encounters for people from the whole region, many of whom have had family members killed during the wars. Some of the groups with whom QPSW is working are human rights organisations, since human rights violations both during the wars and since their formal cessation are rife. The QPSW programme, called 'Dealing with the Past', has found it essential to address human rights as part of the peacebuilding work. Victims of these abuses do not generally think the international standards designed to protect them are a western construct or belong only to one particular religion.

Over a number of years Brian Phillips, a British Friend, has given lectures in the region about human rights and their advocacy. Frequently, although they have heard of the label, many people, including the young and their teachers, seem to be quite ignorant of what the rights actually are, and what they may imply in terms of political, official and private behaviour. As part of her work, QPSW Representative Zorica Trifunovic has been guiding and supporting a human rights advocacy group. As a long-term peace activist, she was and is well-placed to support discussion on what were and are the best opportunities and most effective ways forward in both campaigning and in education as a means of trying to tip the balance of opinion in society. The group has been teaching people that they have a right as citizens to demand something different, both on behalf of themselves and of others, and to demand consistency between word and deed on the part of rulers.

It is important for people to know both what standards their governments have signed up to and paid lip service to, and also to indicate the many cases in which they were simply and indeed arrogantly flouted with impunity. The power-holders would be happy to hold onto their positions as well as to continue with their oppressive and illegal discriminatory behaviour against minority groups. All of this could come under the general description of empowerment, thus contributing to the evolution of attitudes, beliefs and personal ownership of responsibility, as well as commitments by politicians and officials. As Quaker Representatives the team demonstrate in all their work the manifestation of 'that of God' in all people, both those immediately experienced as allies and those immediately experienced as opponents or enemies.

In Uganda, QPSW's programme in the northern city of Gulu has been working with many different groups to end the conflict there, and to promote peacebuilding in the communities torn apart by 20 years of violence. The overriding human right absent here is peace itself, and all QPSW work contributes to that goal. Other human rights abuses here are amongst the worst in the world, used deliberately in the conflict for maximum impact. For example, the Lords Resistance Army (LRA) abducted thousands of children, some as young as 8 or even 2 to be fighters.[4] Every conceivable 'human right' of these children has been violated: taken from their families by force; shot if they did not obey or were too tired, weak or ill to march with the unit; forced to attack their own families, friends and other people in their communities, and to torture, maim or kill them in horrible and grotesque ways. Totally brutalised, these children grew up in the rebel units: the girls raped, becoming sex slaves; the boys who survived becoming themselves rapists, commanders, brutalisers and murderers.

The QPSW programme in Gulu has worked slowly and carefully with a group of girls who had been abducted into the LRA, who had escaped and who wanted to help other children with similar experiences. This group has, through QPSW assistance, not only become successful in helping other children, but has become a recognised non-governmental organisation, received Unicef funding and been visited by Hilary Benn, when he was UK Secretary of State for International Development. At the time of writing there is a ceasefire holding and peace talks in Juba have made unprecedented progress. However, there is still much cynicism, and recognition that true peace might be elusive for years to come. Together with its partners, QPSW is involved in the current debate around how to preserve the rights of those who were abducted by the LRA and are now returning home, whilst also assessing how these rights need to be balanced with the justice and reparation rights of victims, who might have been harmed by those same abductees. There will be a delicate balance of rights played out on the path to peace, and this is being carefully negotiated at present. Linking to this work, the issue of child soldiers has been part of the human rights programme at the Quaker UN Office in Geneva since 1979, and peace in northern Uganda has been given a high profile in New York by the Quaker UN Office there.

Many years ago, a concern about children being used to fight, to kill and to die was tested in the Monthly Meeting of a Friend. It was taken to her Yearly Meeting, thence to Friends World Committee for Consultation, which asked the QUNOs to work on it. Most human rights issues on which QUNO works have similarly come through channels of discernment from concerns at local meetings. QUNO worked on child soldier issues for years, gradually increasing the numbers of other organisations working together and eventually leading to the UN's optional protocol to the Convention on the Rights of the Child on children and armed conflict. QUNO was one of the founders of 'the coalition to stop the use of child soldiers', which has successfully taken up the campaigning, research and advocacy on this issue. Human rights, development and peace organisations are all involved in this international coalition. QUNO has recently started promoting the idea of using restorative justice principles in peacebuilding and transitional justice, and other Quaker experts on this subject have recently produced a paper for the new UN Peacebuilding Commission. It may be that restorative justice is a more appropriate way of addressing the issue of child soldiers who have committed war crimes, rather than seeing this as only an issue of either criminal prosecution through the normal (punitive) processes or non-judicial truth and reconciliation processes.

Does it have to be the Quakers who work on these issues, whether at the UN or at local level? Why should the Religious Society of Friends be involved with these secular 'rights?' From slavery to stopping the British export of leg irons in the 1980s, from child soldiers in Uganda to exploitation of under-18s in the British armed forces, from prison reform and Elizabeth Fry to children of imprisoned mothers today, Quakers do not work alone. Many people of all faiths and none are represented by non-governmental organisations and by diplomats from around the world in the UN fora which consider human rights, and in work on the ground trying to uncover, publicise and rectify abuses. Much of the work involves legal processes and much of it requires considerable expertise. However, it seems that other organisations and indeed victims of human rights abuses not only appreciate the unique Quaker way of working and respect Quaker experience, they also acknowledge the deeply held beliefs which underpin the work, the sense of doing things not for our own advantage, but because they are right.

Notes

1. *Quaker Faith and Practice*, 1995, London: Britain Yearly Meeting, 24.49.
2. Brett, Rachel, 2007, 'Persistent Objectors at the United Nations', *Friends Quarterly* vol. 35, no. 7, July, pp. 301-9.
3. For further details on Quaker work see www.quno.org and www.quaker.org.uk .
4. De Temmerman, Els, 2001, *Aboke Girls*, Kampala, Uganda: Fountain Press.